John Philpot

The sacred tree

The tree in religion and myth

John Philpot

The sacred tree
The tree in religion and myth

ISBN/EAN: 9783337259693

Printed in Europe, USA, Canada, Australia, Japan

Cover: Foto ©Lupo / pixelio.de

More available books at **www.hansebooks.com**

THE SACRED TREE

THE SACRED TREE

OR

THE TREE IN RELIGION AND MYTH

BY

MRS. J. H. PHILPOT

London
MACMILLAN AND CO., Limited
NEW YORK: THE MACMILLAN COMPANY
1897

All rights reserved

PREFACE

THE reader is requested to bear in mind that this volume lays no claim to scholarship, independent research, or originality of view. Its aim has been to select and collate, from sources not always easily accessible to the general reader, certain facts and conclusions bearing upon a subject of acknowledged interest. In so dealing with one of the many modes of primitive religion, it is perhaps inevitable that the writer should seem to exaggerate its importance, and in isolating a given series of data to undervalue the significance of the parallel facts from which they are severed. It is undeniable that the worship of the spirit-inhabited tree has usually, if not always, been linked with, and in many cases overshadowed by other cults; that sun, moon, and stars, sacred springs and stones, holy mountains, and animals of the most diverse kind, have all been approached with singular impartiality by primitive man, as enshrining or symbolising a divine principle. But no other form of pagan ritual has been so widely distributed, has left behind it such persistent traces, or appeals so closely to modern sympathies as the worship of the tree; of none is the study better calculated to throw light on the dark ways of primitive thought, or to arouse general interest in a branch of research which is as vigorous and fruitful as it is new. For these reasons, in spite of obvious disadvantages, its separate treatment has seemed to the writer to be completely justifiable.

CONTENTS

CHAPTER I

TREE-WORSHIP—ITS DISTRIBUTION AND ORIGIN

Primitive conception of the tree-spirit—Illustrations of the evidence for tree-worship: from archaeology, from folk-lore, from literature, from contemporary anthropology—Earliest record of tree-worship, the cylinders of Chaldaea—The symbol of the sacred tree; its development—Meaning of the symbol—Tree-worship amongst the Semites—Canaanitish tree-worship—The *ashéra*—The decoration of the Temple at Jerusalem—Tree-worship in ancient Egypt—The sacred sycamores—Survival of the worship in the Soudan and in Africa generally—Osiris, originally a tree-god; compared with other vegetation spirits—Tammuz, Adonis, Attis, Dionysus—The sacred trees of the Persians—Tree-worship still existent in India; evidence of its ancient prevalence—Its incorporation in Buddhism—Other instances of tree-worship in the East—The evidence from America.
Greek and Roman tree-worship—The German religion of the grove—Persistence of the belief in tree-spirits in Russia, Poland, and Finland—Sacred trees in mediaeval France—The rites of the Druids—Evidence of tree-worship in Saxon England; its survival in May-day customs—General conclusions as to the ancient prevalence of tree-worship—Its origin; views of Robertson Smith, Herbert Spencer, and Grant Allen . . Page 1

CHAPTER II

THE GOD AND THE TREE

Tree-spirits divisible into tree-gods and tree-demons—The gods of antiquity subject to physical limitations, and approachable only through their material embodiment or symbol—This embodiment frequently a tree—The sycamores of Egypt believed to be inhabited by deities—Developments of this conception—In Greece the tree one of the earliest symbols of the god—The chief Greek gods in their origin deities of vegetation—The ritual of the tree—The tree dressed or carved to represent an anthropomorphic god—

Late survival of this custom amongst the classical nations—Its prevalence in other countries.

The god's own tree—Zeus and the oak—Apollo and the laurel—Aphrodite and the myrtle—Athena and the olive—The association of a particular god with a particular tree not known amongst the Semites—The bodhi-trees or trees of wisdom of the Buddhas—The sculptures of Bharhut—Brahma and the golden lotus—The holy basil of India—The grove of Upsala, the home of Woden—Taara and the oak—The great oak at Romove.

Gifts to the tree: in Arabia, in Egypt, in Greece—Dedication of arms, trophies, etc.

The use of branches and wreaths in religious ceremonies—The procession of the sacred bough in Greek festivals—The ceremonial use of branches common throughout the East.

The tree as sanctuary and asylum . Page 24

CHAPTER III

WOOD-DEMONS AND TREE-SPIRITS

General characteristics of the tree-demon—The fabulous monsters of Chaldaea—The *jinni* of Arabia—The hairy monsters of the Bible—The tree-demons of Egypt—The woodland creatures of Greece—Centaurs and cyclops—Pan, satyrs, and sileni—The fauns and silvani of Italy—Female woodland spirits—The hamadryads—Alexander and the flower-maidens—The vine-women of Lucian—Corresponding instances in modern folk-lore—The soul of the nymph actually held to inhabit the tree—The belief that blood would flow when the tree was injured—Examples from Virgil, Ovid, and from modern folk-lore—Indian belief in wood-spirits.

The wood-spirits of Central and North Europe—Their general characteristics—The moss-women—The wild women of Tyrol—The wood-spirits of the Grisons—The white and green ladies—The Swedish tree-spirit—The Russian Ljeschi—The Finnish Tapio—The Tengus of Japan—Wood-demons of Peru and Brazil 52

CHAPTER IV

THE TREE IN ITS RELATION TO HUMAN LIFE

The tree represented as the progenitor of the human race; as related in the Eddas; in Iranian mythology; amongst the Sioux Indians—The classical view—Human beings represented as the fruit of a tree—Individual births from a tree—Mythical births beneath a tree; Zeus; Hermes; Hera; Apollo and Artemis; Romulus and Remus.

Metamorphoses—Apollo and Daphne—Meaning of the legend—The daughters of Clymene—Baucis and Philemon—Other instances of metamorphosis—The growth of flowers from the blood of the dead, or from the tears shed over

them—Transmigration of souls into trees—Tristram and Iseult—Sweet
William and Fair Margaret—Other instances.
The conception of the tree as sympathetically interwoven with human life—The
family tree—The community tree—The fig-tree in the Roman Comitium
—The patrician and plebeian myrtle-trees.
The tree as the symbol of reproductive energy—The Semitic mother-goddess—
Interpretation of the Chaldaean sacred tree as the symbol of fertility—The
tree-inhabiting spirit of vegetation as the patron of fertility—Observances
connected therewith . . . Page 72

CHAPTER V

THE TREE AS ORACLE

The oracular power a corollary to the belief in the tree-inhabiting god—Connection
of the tree-oracle with the earth-oracle—The oracles of the Chaldaeans—
Canaanite tree-oracles—"The tree of the soothsayers"—The oracular oak
of Zeus at Dodona—The oracle of Zeus Ammon—The prophetic laurel of
Delphi—Oracular trees in Armenia, in Arabia—Alexander the Great and
the Persian tree-oracles—The prophetic ilex grove at Rome—Other Italian
tree-oracles: at Tibur; at Preneste—Tree-omens—Legends of speaking
trees—Oracle-lots—The origin of the divining-rod—Cut rods believed
to retain some of the divine power resident in the tree—The life-rood—
The divining-rod a survival of the tree-oracle—Its modern use—Divination
by roots and leaves 93

CHAPTER VI

THE UNIVERSE-TREE

Wide distribution of the conception—Its plausibility to the primitive mind;
especially to the inhabitants of level countries—Earliest version of the
world-tree found in an Accadian hymn of great antiquity—Probably a
poetical amplification of the sacred spirit-inhabited tree—The world-tree
and the world-mountain—The two conceptions combined in the Norse
Yggdrasil, as described in the Eddas—Indian and Persian versions of the
world-tree—Buddhist development of the idea—The cosmogony of the
Phoenicians—Egyptian variants; the Tât-pillar; the golden gem-bearing
tree of the sky—Traces of the world-tree in Chinese and Japanese mythology—A similar tradition amongst North American Indians.
The Eastern conception of the stars as fruits of the world-tree, and as jewels
hung thereon—A motive common in Oriental art—The golden apples of the
Hesperides—Other instances of the world-tree in European legend—
The monster oak of the Kalevala—Corresponding tradition amongst the
Esthonians.

The food of the gods, a conception associated with that of the world-tree—The Persian haoma, a mystical tree, producing an immortalising juice—Its terrestrial counterpart; the haoma sacrament—The Vedic soma; not only a plant but a powerful deity—Identification of the plant—De Gubernatis on the soma ritual—The effect of the soma drink—Corresponding conceptions amongst the Greeks—Origin of the idea . Page 109

CHAPTER VII

PARADISE

Varieties of the tradition: (1) as the seat of the gods; (2) as the home of the first parents; (3) as the abode of the blessed—All associated with the conception of a mystical tree, in itself an idealisation of the spirit-inhabited tree worshipped on earth—The paradise of the gods in Indian tradition; its five miraculous trees—The paradise of Genesis and of the Persian sacred books—The tree of paradise compared with sacred cedar of Chaldaea—paradise as the abode of the blessed, a post-exilic tradition amongst the Jews—The paradise of the Talmud; and of the Koran—The confusion in the ancient traditions of paradise partly due to a limited conception of space and to a belief in the propinquity of heaven—Greek conceptions of paradise—Milton's description influenced by ancient traditions of an elevated paradise.

The earthly paradise—Persistence of the tradition; Sir John Maundeville's version—Icelandic tradition—The lost Atlantis of Plato a variant of the paradise legend—St. Brandan and the Isle of Avalon—Christopher Columbus—Japanese tradition of an island of eternal youth, with its marvellous tree—Developments of the idea of the tree of paradise—Its representation in art 128

CHAPTER VIII

MAY CELEBRATIONS

Their ancient religious significance—The old English May-day—Fetching in the May—Puritan condemnation of the May-poles—Their removal "as a heathenish vanity"—Existing survivals of May customs—May-day rhymes.

Origin of the celebrations: 1. The bringing in of the May-bough—Wide distribution of the custom an evidence of its antiquity—Its original intention—"The May" related to the harvest-bush of France and Western Germany, and to the Greek *eiresione*—Their common purpose, to bring to the house a share of the blessings assumed to be at the disposal of the tree-inhabiting spirit.

2. The May-pole: its primitive intention to bring to the village, as the May-bough to the family, the newly-quickened generative potency resident in the

woods—Wide prevalence of the custom—Association of the May-pole with a human image or doll, representing the vegetation spirit—The Greek festival of the little Daedala—The May-pole, originally renewed every year, became later a permanent erection, newly dressed on May-day—Assumed beneficent influence of the May-pole.

3. The May Queen, May Lady, or King and Queen of the May: Evidence that these personages were originally regarded as human representatives or embodiments of the generalised tree-soul—Often associated with its vegetable representative, the tree or bough; or clothed in leaves and flowers, *e.g.* the Green George of Carinthia and our Jack-in-the-Green—The custom general throughout Europe—Robin Hood and Maid Marian originally King and Queen of the May—In primitive times the human representative of the vegetation spirit probably sacrificed, in order that the spirit might pass to a more vigorous successor—Human sacrifice in Mexico—Survival in symbol of this ancient custom in Bavaria, Swabia, Saxony, etc.

Page 144

CHAPTER IX

CHRISTMAS OBSERVANCES

Distinctly pagan in their origin, and adapted to Christian use under the influence of the Church—The Roman Saturnalia—The use of mistletoe a direct legacy from the Druids—The decoration of the house with evergreens also a Druidic custom.

The Christmas-tree; its introduction into England extremely recent; not universally established in Germany, the land of its origin, until the present century—References to it by Goethe and Schiller—Earliest record from Strasburg about 1600 A.D.—Theological disapproval—Theories as to its origin—Probably connected with the legend of Christmas flowering trees—Examples—The Glastonbury thorn—Mannhardt's view; a decorated tree the recognised scenic symbol of Christmas in the paradise play of the Middle Ages, wherein the story of the Fall was dramatically associated with that of the Nativity—An ancient German custom to force into flower boughs cut on a sacred night during the great autumn festival—The date of severance delayed under priestly influence so that the boughs might flower at Christmas—Instances of the survival of this custom—The lights on the Christmas-tree a comparatively recent innovation—Legends of light-bearing trees—The lights possibly derived from ancient solstitial observances—The Christmas-tree an illustration of the blending of pagan and mediaeval ideas —A point in which the many phases of tree-worship converge . 162

INDEX . . . 175

ILLUSTRATIONS

FIG.		PAGE
Sacred tree with its supporters, from St. Mark's, Venice		*Frontispiece*
1, 2, 3. Rudimentary and conventionalised forms of the sacred tree		5
4. Sacred tree with its supporters, surmounted by the winged disc, from an Assyrian cylinder		6
5. Sacred tree, from the Temple of Athena at Pryene		
6. The same, from a sculptured slab in the Treasury of St. Mark's, Venice		7
7. A *Ba* or soul receiving the lustral water from a tree-goddess		10
8. Sacred tree with worshippers, from eastern gateway at Sânchi		15
9. Sacred tree, from a Mexican manuscript		17
10. The goddess Nûit in her sacred sycamore bestowing the bread and water of the next world		26
11. Sacred tree of Dionysus, with a statue of the god and offerings		27
12. Sacred pine of Silvanus, with a bust of the god, and votive gifts		28
13. Fruit-tree dressed as Dionysus		31
14, 15. Forms of the Tât or Didû, the emblem of Osiris		34
16. Apollo on his sacred tripod, a laurel branch in his hand		36
17. Coin of Athens, of the age of Pericles or earlier, showing olive spray		38
18. Coin of Athens, third century B.C.		38
19. The Bodhi-tree of Kanaka Muni		41

FIG.		PAGE
20.	Wild elephants paying their devotions to the sacred banian of Kâsyapa Buddha .	42
21.	Sacred sycamore, with offerings	44
22.	Sacred tree of Artemis, hung with weapons of the chase .	45
23.	Sacred laurel of Apollo at Delphi, adorned with fillets and votive tablets; beneath it the god appearing to protect Orestes .	50
24.	Imperial coin of Myra in Lycia, showing tree-goddess	87
25.	Sacred tree and worshipper, from a Chaldaean cylinder	88
26.	Sacred tree as symbol of fertility, from an Assyrian bas-relief	89
27.	Yggdrasil, the Scandinavian world-tree	115
28.	From a Babylonian seal	130

CHAPTER I

TREE-WORSHIP—ITS DISTRIBUTION AND ORIGIN

It is the purpose of the present volume to deal as concisely as possible with the many religious observances, popular customs, legends, traditions and ideas which have sprung from or are related to the primitive conception of the tree-spirit. There is little doubt that most if not all races, at some period of their development, have regarded the tree as the home, haunt, or embodiment of a spiritual essence, capable of more or less independent life and activity, and able to detach itself from its material habitat and to appear in human or in animal form. This belief has left innumerable traces in ancient art and literature, has largely shaped the usages and legends of the peasantry, and impressed its influence on the ritual of almost all the primitive religions of mankind. There is, indeed, scarcely a country in the world where the tree has not at one time or another been approached with reverence or with fear, as being closely connected with some spiritual potency.

The evidence upon which this assertion is based is overwhelming in amount, and is frequently to be found in quarters where until lately its presence was unsuspected or its significance ignored. For instance, in the interior of that fascinating storehouse of antiquity, St. Mark's at Venice, there are embedded in the walls, high above one's head, a number of ancient sculptured slabs, on each of which a conventionalised plant, with foliage most truthfully and lovingly rendered, is set between two fabulous monsters, as fantastic and impossible as any supporters to be met with in the whole range of heraldry (see Frontispiece). To the ordinary observer these strange sculptures say nothing; probably he passes over them lightly, as the offspring of that quaint mediaeval fancy which was so prolific in monstrous births. But the student of Oriental art at once detects in them a familiar design, a design whose pedigree can be traced back to the day, six thousand years ago, when the Chaldaean Semites were taking their culture and religion from the old Accadians who dwelt on the shores of the Persian Gulf. In the central plant he recognises the symbol or ideograph of a divine attribute or activity, if not a representation of the visible embodiment or abode of a god, and in the raised hand or forepaw of the supporters he discerns the conventional attitude of adoration. The design, in short, which was probably handed on from Assyria to Persia, and from Persia to Byzantium, and so to Venice, is a vestige of that old world religion which regarded the tree as one of the sacred haunts of deity.

Again, the same conception, the record of which is thus strangely preserved in the very fabric of a Christian edifice, is to be traced with equal certainty in the older and scarcely less permanent fabric of popular tradition and custom. The folk-lore of the modern European peasant, and the observances with which Christmas, May-day, and the gathering of the harvest are still celebrated in civilised countries, are all permeated by the primitive idea that there was a spiritual essence embodied in vegetation, that trees, like men, had spirits, passing in and out amongst them, which possessed a mysterious and potent influence over human affairs, and which it was therefore wise and necessary to propitiate.

A third example of the less recondite evidence on the subject is to be found in the Book that we all know best. When we once realise how deeply rooted and time-honoured was the belief that there was a spiritual force inherent in vegetation, we cease to wonder at the perversity with which the less cultured Israelites persisted in planting groves and setting up altars under every green tree. Read in the light of modern research, the Old Testament presents a drama of surpassing interest, a record of internecine struggle between the aspiration of the few towards the worship of a single, omnipresent, unconditioned God and the conservative adhesion of the many to the primitive ritual and belief common to all the Semitic tribes. For the backsliding children of Israel were no more idolaters, in the usual meaning of the word, than were the Canaanites whose rites they imitated. Their view of nature was that of the primitive Semite, if not of the primitive man. All parts of nature, in their idea, were full of spiritual forces, more or less, but never completely, detached in their movements and action from the material objects to which they were supposed properly to belong. "In ritual the sacred object was spoken of and treated as the god himself; it was not merely his symbol, but his embodiment, the permanent centre of his activity, in the same sense in which the human body is the permanent centre of man's activity. The god inhabited the tree or sacred stone not in the sense in which a man inhabits a house, but in the sense in which his soul inhabits his body."[1]

To the three classes of evidence, derived respectively from archæology, from folk-lore, and from ancient literature, which have been thus briefly exemplified, may be added a fourth, equally important and prolific, that namely of contemporary anthropology. Scarcely a book is printed on the customs of uncivilised races which does not contribute some new fact to the subject. The illustration of an Arab praying to a tree, in Slatin Pasha's recently published volume, is no surprise to the anthropologist, who has learnt to look for such survivals of primitive customs wherever culture still remains primitive.

Now of all primitive customs and beliefs there is none which has a greater claim upon our interest than the worship of the tree, for there is none which has had a wider distribution throughout the world, or has left a deeper impress on the traditions and observances of mankind. Its antiquity is undoubted, for when history begins to speak, we find it already firmly established amongst the oldest civilised races. What is probably its earliest record is met with on the engraved cylinders of Chaldaea, some of which date back to 4000 B.C. Even at that period it would appear that the Chaldaeans had advanced beyond the stage of crude tree-worship, as found to this day amongst uncivilised races, for the sacred tree had already undergone a process of idealisation. In a bilingual hymn, which is of Accadian origin, and probably one of

---

[1] Robertson Smith, *Religion of the Semites* (Edin. 1889), p. 84.

the most ancient specimens of literature in existence, a mystical tree is described as the abode of the gods. And it was probably by a similar process of idealisation that a conventional representation of the sacred tree came to be one of the most important symbols of Chaldaean religion. This symbol, which we have already seen in decorative use on the slabs at St. Mark's, appears on the oldest Chaldaean cylinders "as a stem divided at the base, surmounted by a fork or a crescent, and cut, midway, by one or more cross bars which sometimes bear a fruit at each extremity.

FIG. 1.   FIG. 2.   FIG. 3.

Rudimentary and conventionalised forms of the sacred tree.

(From Chaldaean and Assyrian cylinders. Goblet d'Alviella.)

This rudimentary image frequently changes into the palm, the pomegranate, the cypress, vine, etc.[1] On the Assyrian monuments of about 1000 B.C. and later, the figure becomes still more complex and more artistically conventionalised, and it nearly always stands between two personages facing each other, who are sometimes priests or kings in an attitude of adoration, sometimes monstrous creatures, such as are so often met with in Assyro-Chaldaean imagery, lions, sphinxes, griffins, unicorns, winged bulls, men or *genii* with the head of an eagle, and so forth. Above it is frequently sus-

[1] Goblet d'Alviella, *The Migration of Symbols* (London, 1894), p. 119.

pended the winged circle, personifying the supreme deity." In his exhaustive chapter on this ancient design, M. Goblet d'Alviella has shown that it obtained a wide dissemination throughout the world, and is used even to this day in the fictile and textile art of the East.[1] M. Menant concludes from his exhaustive study of the cylinders, that the worship of the sacred tree in Assyria was intimately associated with that of the supreme deity, its symbol being incontestably one of the most sacred emblems of the Assyrian religion.[2] M. Lenormant's view was that the winged

FIG. 4.—Sacred tree with its supporters, surmounted by the winged disc.
(From an Assyrian cylinder. Goblet d'Alviella.)

FIG. 5.—Sacred tree, much conventionalised.
(From a capital of the Temple of Athena at Pryene. Goblet d'Alviella.)

circle, in conjunction with the sacred tree, represented the primeval cosmogonic pair, the creative sun and the fertile earth, and was a symbol of the divine mystery of generation.[3] In Babylonia the sacred tree was no doubt closely associated with Istar, the divine mother, who was originally not a Semitic, but an Accadian goddess, and whose cult, together with that of her bridegroom Tammuz, was introduced into Chaldaea from Eridu, a city which flourished on the shores of

[1] *Op. cit.* chap. iv.
[2] J. Menant, *Les Pierres gravées de la Haute-Asie* (Paris, 1886), Part II. p. 63.
[3] *Les Origines de l'Histoire* (Paris, 1888), vol. i. p. 88.

the Persian Gulf between 3000 and 4000 B.C.[1] That the Accadians were familiar with the worship of the tree may also be inferred from the fact that their chief god, Ea, was closely associated with the sacred cedar, on whose core his name was supposed to be inscribed.

But however much their attitude towards the sacred tree may have been modified under Accadian influence, the Chaldaeans in their worship of the tree

FIG. 6.—Sacred tree, from a sculptured slab in the Treasury of St. Mark's, Venice.

only followed the rule of their Semitic kindred, for "the conception of trees as demoniac beings was familiar to all the Semites, and the tree was adored as divine in every part of the Semitic area."[2] Even that stationary Semite, the modern Arab, holds certain trees inviolable as being inhabited by spirits, and honours them with sacrifices and decorations, and to this day the traveller in Palestine sometimes lights upon holy trees hung with tokens of homage.

[1] A. H. Sayce, *Religion of the Ancient Babylonians* (London, 1887), Lect. IV.
[2] Robertson Smith, *op. cit.* p. 169.

This strange persistence of a primitive religion in the very birthplace of a most exalted spiritual worship is an additional evidence of its remarkable vitality. For there is no country in the world where the tree was ever more ardently worshipped than it was in ancient Palestine. Amongst the Canaanites every altar to the god had its sacred tree beside it, and when the Israelites established local sanctuaries under their influence, they set up their altar under a green tree, and planted beside it as its indispensable accompaniment an *ashéra*, which was either a living tree or a tree-like post, and not a "grove," as rendered in the Authorised Version. This *ashéra* was undoubtedly worshipped as a sacred symbol of the deity. Originally it appears to have been associated with Ashtoreth or Astarte, the Syrian Istar, the revolting character of whose worship perhaps explains the excessive bitterness of the biblical denunciations.[1] But the *ashéra* was also erected by the altars of other gods, and in pre-prophetic days even beside that of Jehovah Himself, whence it may be concluded that "in early times tree-worship had such a vogue in Canaan, that the sacred tree or the pole, its surrogate, had come to be viewed as a *general* symbol of deity."[2] The great antiquity of the cult in Syria was recognised in the local traditions, for an old Phoenician cosmogony, quoted by Eusebius, states that "the first men consecrated the plants shooting out of the earth, and judged them gods, and worshipped them, and made meat and drink offerings to them."[3] In addition to the *ashéra*, the Chaldaean symbol of the sacred tree between its

---

[1] Cf. Ex. xxxiv. 13; Deut. vii. 5, xii. 3, xvi. 21; Judges iii. 7, vi. 25; 1 Kings xiv. 15; 2 Kings xvii. 16; cf. also Isaiah i. 29, lxv. 3, lxvi. 17.

[2] Robertson Smith, *op. cit.* p. 172.
[3] Eusebius, *Praepar. Evang.*, lib. i. cap. 10.

supporters was also familiar to the Phoenicians, and is found wherever their art penetrated, notably in Cyprus and on the archaic pottery of Corinth and Athens.[1] It is highly probable that both these sacred symbols had a common origin, but the connection must have been lost sight of in later times, for we find Ezekiel, to whom the prophetic denunciations of the *ashêra* must have been familiar, decorating the temple of his vision with designs evidently derived from the Chaldaean sacred tree, "a palm-tree between a cherub and a cherub."[2] A similar ornamentation with palm-trees and cherubim, it will be remembered, had been used in the temple built by Solomon.[3]

Amongst the ancient Egyptians, whose "exuberant piety" required, according to M. Maspero, "an actual rabble of gods" to satisfy it, trees were enthusiastically worshipped, side by side with other objects, as the homes of various divinities. The splendid green sycamores, which flourish here and there as though by miracle on the edge of the cultivated land, their rootlets bathed by the leakage of the Nile, were accounted divine and earnestly worshipped by Egyptians of every rank, in the belief that they were animated by spirits, who on occasion could emerge from them. They were habitually honoured with fruit offerings, and the charitable found an outlet for their benevolence in daily replenishing the water-jars placed beneath them for the use of the passer-by, who in his turn would express his gratitude for the boon by reciting a prayer to the deity of the tree. The most famous of these sycamores—the sycamore of the South—was regarded as the living body of Hāthor upon earth;

---

[1] Goblet d'Alviella, *op. cit.* p. 125.   [2] Ezek. xli. 18.
[3] 1 Kings vi. 29-35.

and the tree at Metairieh, commonly called the Tree of the Virgin, is probably the successor of a sacred tree of Heliopolis, in which a goddess, perhaps Hāthor, was worshipped.[1] The district around Memphis was known as the Land of the Sycamore, and contained several trees generally believed to be inhabited by detached doubles of Nûit and Hāthor. Similar trees

FIG. 7.—A *Ba* or soul receiving the lustral water from a tree-goddess.
(From a painting discovered by Prof. Petrie at Thebes. *Illustrated London News*, 25th July 1896.)

are worshipped at the present day both by Christian and Mussulman fellahin.

On the outskirts of the province of Darfur the Bedeyat Arabs, though surrounded by Moslem tribes, still adhere to the same primitive cult. Under the wide-spreading branches of an enormous heglik-tree, and on a spot kept beautifully clean and sprinkled

[1] G. Maspero, *The Dawn of Civilisation* (London, 1894), p. 122.

with fine sand, they beseech an unknown god to direct them in their undertakings and to protect them from danger.[1] They have, in short, retained, in spite of the pressure of Islamism, the old heathen worship which still widely prevails amongst the uncivilised races of the African continent. Thus on the Guinea Coast almost every village has its sacred tree, and in some parts offerings are still made to them. The negroes of the Congo plant a sacred tree before their houses and set jars of palm-wine under it for the tree-spirit.[2] In Dahomey prayers and gifts are offered to trees in time of sickness. One of the goddesses of the Fantis has her abode in huge cotton-trees. In the Nyassa country, where the spirits of the dead are worshipped as gods, the ceremonies are conducted and offerings placed not at the grave of the dead man, but at the foot of the tree which grows before his house, or if that be unsuitable, beneath some especially beautiful tree selected for the purpose.[3]

To return to ancient Egypt, there is evidence that the great Osiris was originally a tree-god. According to Egyptian mythology, after he had been murdered his coffin was discovered enclosed in a tree-trunk, and he is spoken of in the inscriptions as "the one in the tree," "the solitary one in the acacia." The rites, too, by which his death and burial were annually celebrated appear to couple him closely with Tammuz, Adonis, Attis, Dionysus, and other gods whose worship was associated with a similar ritual.[4] Mr. Frazer, following Mannhardt, contends that all these deities were tree-gods, and that the ceremonial connected with their

---

[1] Slatin Pasha, *Fire and Sword in the Sudan* (London, 1896), p. 114.
[2] J. G. Frazer, *The Golden Bough* (London, 1890), vol. i. p. 60.
[3] Duff Macdonald, *Africana* (London, 1882), vol. i. p. 60.
[4] Frazer, *op. cit.* vol. i. p. 307.

worship was symbolical of the annual death and revival of vegetation. It is certainly true that in Babylonia, Egypt, Phoenicia, and above all in Phrygia, a peculiarly emotional form of worship, which subsequently extended to Cyprus, Crete, Greece, and Italy, arose in connection with deities who were closely associated with vegetable life. Tammuz—

> Whose annual wound in Lebanon allured
> The Syrian damsels to lament his fate,

and for whose resuscitation his bride, the goddess Istar, descended into Hades—was represented as originally dwelling in a tree.[1] Adonis, who was the beloved of Aphrodite—the Syrian Astarte—and is Tammuz under another name, was born from a myrrh-tree. Attis, the favourite of Cybele, who was worshipped with barbarous rites in Phrygia, was represented in the form of a decorated pine-tree, to which his image was attached. Dionysus, whose death and resurrection were celebrated in Crete and elsewhere, was worshipped throughout Greece as "Dionysus of the Tree." These facts are sufficient to warrant the inference that tree-worship was very firmly rooted in those regions where the Semitic races came into contact with the Aryans. In Phrygia it was peculiarly prominent, as we know from classical references. The archaeological evidence is vague and incomplete, but a characteristic device frequent in Phrygian art, in which two animals, usually lions rampant, face one another on either side of a pillar, or an archaic representation of the mother-goddess Cybele,[2] recalls the sacred tree of Babylonia. The device is familiar in connection

---

[1] A. H. Sayce, *op. cit.* p. 238.
[2] *Encyclop. Brit.*, 9th edition, vol. xviii. p. 850.

with the lion-gate of Mycenae, which was probably erected under Phrygian influence.

The Persians venerated trees as the dwelling-place of the deity, as the haunts of good and evil spirits, and as the habitations in which the souls of heroes and of the virtuous dead continued their existence. According to Plutarch, they assigned some trees and plants to the good God, others to the evil demon.[1] The Zend-Avesta ordained that the trees which Ormuzd had given should be prayed to as pure and holy, and adored with fire and lustral water;[2] and according to tradition, when Zoroaster died, Ormuzd himself translated his soul into a lofty tree, and planted it upon a high mountain. The cypress was regarded by the Persians as especially sacred. It was closely associated with fire-worship, and was revered as a symbol of the pure light of Ormuzd. It is frequently represented on ancient gravestones in conjunction with the lion, the symbol of the sun-god Mithra.[3] Another venerated tree was the myrtle, a branch of which was used as an essential accompaniment in all religious functions. The observances connected with the Persian worship of the Haoma plant will be dealt with in a later chapter. The Achaemenian kings regarded the plane as their peculiar tree, and a representation of it in gold formed part of their state. A certain plane-tree in Lydia was presented by Xerxes with vessels of gold and costly apparel, and committed to the guardianship of one of his "immortals."[4]

In India, where tree-worship once enjoyed a wide prevalence, it has left indubitable traces on the

[1] *Isis et Osiris*, 46.
[2] Lajard, *Le Culte du cyprès pyramidal* (1845), p. 148.
[3] Sir. W. Ouseley, *Travels* (London, 1819), vol. iii. p. 83.
[4] Herodotus, vii. 31.

religions which displaced it, and it is still encountered in its crudest form amongst some of the aboriginal hill tribes. The Garrows, for instance, who possess neither temples nor altars, set up a bamboo before their huts, and sacrifice before it to their deity.[1] On a mountain in Travancore there existed until quite recently an ancient tree, which was regarded by the natives as the residence of a powerful deity. Sacrifices were offered to it, and sermons preached before it; it served, indeed, as the cathedral of the district. At length, to the horror of its worshippers, an English missionary had it cut down and used in the construction of a chapel on its site.[2] The ancient prevalence of tree-worship in India is established by frequent references to sacred trees in the Vedas, and by the statement of Q. Curtius that the companions of Alexander the Great noticed that the Indians "reputed as gods whatever they held in reverence, especially trees, which it was death to injure."[3] This ancient reverence for the tree was recognised by Buddhism, and adapted to its more advanced mode of thought. The asvattha or pippala-tree, *Ficus Religiosa*, which had previously been identified with the supreme deity, Brahma, came to be venerated above all others by the special injunction of Gautama, as that under which he had achieved perfect knowledge.[4] In his previous incarnations Gautama himself is represented as having been a tree-spirit no less than forty-three times. The evidence of the monuments as to the importance attached to the tree in early Buddhism is equally definite. The Sânchi and Ama-ravati sculptures, some

---

[1] R. Folkard, *Plant-lore, Legends, and Lyrics* (London, 1892), p. 239.
[2] M. D. Conway, *Demonology and Devil-lore* (London, 1879), vol. i. p. 299.
[3] Quintus Curtius, *De Gestis Alex.* viii. 33.
[4] Folkard, *op. cit.* p. 4.

casts of which are in the British Museum, contain representations of the sacred tree decorated with garlands and surrounded by votaries, whilst the worship of the trees identified with the various Buddhas is repeatedly represented on the Stûpa of Bharhut.

There is very little evidence of the existence of tree-worship amongst the Chinese, but they have a

FIG. 8.—Sacred tree with worshippers, from eastern gateway of Buddhist Tope at Sânchi.
(Fergusson's *Tree and Serpent Worship* (1868), Plate xxv.)

tradition of a Tree of Life, and of a drink of immortality made from various sacred plants. They also make use of the divining-rod, which is an offshoot of tree-worship, and certain Taoist medals, like the talismans worn in Java, bear the familiar symbol of the sacred tree.[1] In Japan certain old trees growing near Shinto temples are regarded as sacred, and

[1] Goblet d'Alviella, *op. cit.* p. 130.

bound with a fillet of straw rope, "as if they were tenanted by a divine spirit."[1] Japanese mythology tells of holy *sakaki* trees growing on the Mountain of Heaven, and of a herb of immortality to be gathered on the Island of Eternal Youth.

Amongst the semi-civilised races which border upon these ancient states the tree is still almost universally regarded as the dwelling-place of a spirit, and as such is protected, venerated, and often presented with offerings. In Sumatra and Borneo certain old trees are held to be sacred, and the Dyaks would regard their destruction as an impious act. The Mintira of the Malay Peninsula believe that trees are inhabited by terrible spirits capable of inflicting diseases. The Talein of Burmah never cut down a tree without a prayer to the indwelling spirit. The Siamese have such veneration for the takhien-tree that they offer it cakes and rice before felling it; so strong, indeed, is their dread of destroying trees of any kind, and thereby offending the gods inhabiting them, that all necessary tree-felling is relegated to the lowest criminals. Even at the present day they frequently make offerings to the tree-dwelling spirits, and hang gifts on any tree whose deity they desire to propitiate.[2]

In the Western Hemisphere, the fact that the drawing of a tree with two opposed personages or supporters, similar in design to the sacred tree of the Chaldaeans, has been found in an ancient Mexican MS., has been put forward as an additional argument in favour of the pre-Columbian colonisation of that continent and its early contact with the Eastern world.[3]

---

[1] Murray's *Handbook for Japan* (London, 1884), p. 66. (London, 1871), vol. ii. pp. 196, 198.

[2] E. B. Tylor, *Primitive Culture* [3] Goblet d'Alviella, *op. cit.* p. 131.

Speaking generally, however, the worship of the tree appears to have flourished less widely in the New World than the Old, though traces of it have been found all over the continent.[1] A large ash-tree is regarded with great veneration by the Indians of Lake Superior, and in Mexico there was a cypress, the spreading branches of which were loaded by the natives with votive offerings, locks of hair, teeth, and morsels of ribbon; it was many centuries old, and had probably had mysterious influence ascribed to it, and been decorated with offerings long before the discovery of America.[2] By that date, however, the Mexicans had apparently advanced beyond the earliest stage of religious development, and expanded the idea of individual tree-spirits into the more general conception of a god of vegetation. It was in the honour of such a god that their May-Day celebrations were held and their human sacrifices offered. In Nicaragua cereals were worshipped as well as trees. In more primitive Patagonia the cruder form of worship persists, a certain tree standing upon a hill being still resorted to by numerous worshippers, each of whom brings his offering.

Fig. 9.—From a Mexican manuscript.
(Goblet d'Alviella.)

To return nearer home, the worship of the tree has prevailed at one time or another in every country of Europe. It played a vital part in the religion of

---

[1] Müller, *Amerikanische Urreligionen* (Basel, 1855), p. 494.

[2] E. B. Tylor, *Anahuac* (London, 1861), pp. 215, 265.

Greece and Rome, and classical literature is full of traditions and ideas which can have been derived from no other source. The subject has been exhaustively treated by Bötticher in his *Baumkultus der Hellenen*.[1] Mr. Farnell, in his recently published work, says that in the earliest period of Greek religion of which we have any record, the tree was worshipped as the shrine of the divinity that housed within it; hence the epithet ἔνδενδρος, applied to Zeus, and the legend of Helene Dendritis.[2] Discoveries made in Crete and the Peloponnese within the present year (1896) seem to show that the worship of deities in aniconic shape as stone pillars or as trees played a great part in the religion of the Mycenaean period about 1500 B.C.[3] The persistent belief of the Greek and Roman peasantry in the existence and power of the various woodland spirits is also vitally connected with the primitive idea of the tree-soul.

In the centre of Europe, covered as it once was with dense forest, the veneration of the tree tinctured all the religious usages of the primitive inhabitants. In ancient Germany, the universal ceremonial religion of the people had its abode in the "*grove*," and the earliest efforts of the Christian missionaries were directed towards the destruction of these venerated woods, or their consecration by the erection within them of a Christian edifice.[4] But long after their nominal conversion the Germans continued to people every wood with spirits, and the legends and folk-lore of their modern descendants are still rich in memories

---

[1] Carl Bötticher, *Der Baumkultus der Hellenen* (Berlin, 1856).
[2] L. R. Farnell, *The Cults of the Greek States* (Oxford, 1896), vol. i. p. 14.
[3] Arthur Evans, in the anthropological section of the British Association, *Times*, 23rd Sept. 1896.
[4] Jacob Grimm, *Deutsche Mythologie* (Göttingen, 1844), vol. i. p. 60.

of this time-honoured superstition. Some of these wood-inhabiting spirits were favourable to man, ready to befriend and help him in difficulty; others were malicious and vindictive. The whole subject has been studied in Germany with characteristic thoroughness, the standard work being Mannhardt's well-known and fascinating *Wald- und Feldkulte*.[1]

In Poland trees appear to have been worshipped as late as the fourteenth century, and in parts of Russia the power of the tree-spirit over the herds was so firmly held, that it was long customary to propitiate it by the sacrifice of a cow. The Permians, a tribe related to the Finns, worshipped trees, among other things, until their conversion to Christianity about 1380 A.D.[2] In parts of Esthonia the peasants even within the present century regarded certain trees as sacred, carefully protected them, hung them with wreaths, and once a year poured fresh bullock's blood about their roots, in order that the cattle might thrive.[3] In the remoter parts of the Czar's domain the belief in tree-demons still persists. They are held to be enormous creatures, who can change their stature at will, and whose voice is heard in the clash of the storm as they spring from tree to tree. In Finland the oak is still called "God's tree," and to this day the birch and the mountain-ash are held sacred by the peasants, and planted beside their cottages with every sign of reverence.

In France at Massilia (now Marseilles) human sacrifices were, in primitive times, offered to trees.[4]

---

[1] *Der Baumkultus der Germanen und ihrer Nachbarstamme* (Berlin, 1875); *Antike Wald- und Feldkulte* (Berlin, 1877). These volumes will be referred to as Mannhardt I. and II.

[2] A. Castrén, *Ethnologische Vorlesungen* (St. Petersburg, 1857), p. 141.

[3] Boecler, *Der Ehsten abergläubische Gebräuche*, etc. (St. Petersburg, 1854), quoted in Fergusson's *Tree and Serpent Worship*.

[4] Lucan, *Pharsalia*, iii. 405.

In the fourth century of our era there was a famous pear-tree at Auxerre which was hung with trophies of the chase and paid all the veneration due to a god.[1] In the life of St. Amandus mention is made of sacred groves and trees worshipped near Beauvais, and various Church councils in the early middle ages denounced those who venerated trees, one held at Nantes in 895 A.D. expressly enjoining the destruction of trees which were consecrated to demons. Traces of the ancient worship still survive here as elsewhere in popular custom; in the south of France they have a graceful observance, in which the spirit of vegetation is personified by a youth clad in green, who feigning sleep is awakened by a maiden's kiss.

In our own islands, as every one knows, the oak-tree played a salient part in the old Druidical worship, and Pliny[2] even derives the name Druid from δρῦς, an oak, as some still connect it with *darach*, the Celtic word for that tree. The important rites with which the mistletoe was severed from the parent tree and dedicated at the altar furnish evidence of the veneration paid to the spirit of the tree, who, according to the teaching of the Druids, retreated into the parasite-bough when the oak leaves withered. The Teutons no doubt brought with them to Britain the religion of the sacred grove, and we find King Edgar condemning the idle rites in connection with the alder and other trees, and Cañute fifty years later forbidding the worship entirely.[3] The ceremonies once connected with the worship of the tree survived in the form of a picturesque symbolism long after their origin had been forgotten. In 1515, at a Twelfth-Night pageant

---

[1] Jacob Grimm, *op. cit.* vol. i. p. 67.
[2] Pliny, *Nat. Hist.* lib. xvi. 95.
[3] Mannhardt I. p. 70.

held at his palace of Greenwich by order of Henry VIII., tree-spirits represented by "VIII wylde-men, all apparayled in grene mosse sodainly came oute of a place lyke a wood" and engaged in battle with the royal knights.[1] It was also a custom of this king in the early years of his reign to resort to the woods with a richly-apparelled retinue in order "to fetche May or grene bows,"—the spirit of vegetation, whose renewed vigour was symbolised, unconsciously no doubt, in the green boughs with which the courtiers decked their caps.[2] May-day ceremonies to celebrate the new life in the forest can be traced in England as far back as the thirteenth century, and the importance still attached to them by the people as late as the seventeenth century is indicated by the rancour with which the Puritans attacked the Maypole, "a heathenish vanity greatly abused to superstition and wickedness." These and other survivals will be more fully treated in a later chapter, and are only mentioned here as showing the ancient prevalence of a belief in tree-spirits, which indeed is alone competent to account for such customs.

In fine, no one who has not studied the subject can have any idea of the sanctity associated with the tree amongst pre-Christian nations. The general conclusion which Bötticher gives as the result of his elaborate research, is that the worship of the tree was not only the earliest form of divine ritual, but was the last to disappear before the spread of Christianity; it existed long before the erection of temples and statues to the gods, flourished side by side with them, and persisted long after they had disappeared.[3] Mr. Tylor, with greater caution, concludes that *direct and*

---

[1] Hall's *Chronicle* (London, 1809), p. 580.
[2] *Ibid.* pp. 515, 520.
[3] Bötticher, *op. cit.* p. 534.

absolute tree-worship may lie very wide and deep in the early history of religion, but that apart from this "there is a wide range of animistic conceptions connected with tree and forest worship. The tree may be the spirit's perch, or shelter, or favourite haunt; or may serve as a scaffold or altar, where offerings can be set out for some spiritual being; or its shelter may be a place of worship set apart by nature, of some tribes the only temple, of many tribes, perhaps, the earliest; or lastly, it may be merely a sacred object patronised by, or associated with, or symbolising some divinity."[1] These varied conceptions, Mr. Tylor thinks, conform, in spite of their confusion, to the animistic theology in which they all have their essential principles.

To discuss the origin of tree-worship would involve the consideration of the whole question of primitive culture, the theory of animism, and the subject of ancestor worship, together with a digression on the very obscure problem of totemism. The last word has not yet been said on these questions, and the time has certainly not yet come to say it. As will be shown in the next two chapters, the general conception of the tree-spirit includes at least two different series of ideas, that on the one hand of the tree-god, whose worship became organised into a definite religion, and on the other hand that of the tree-demons or tree-spirits, whose propitiation was degraded into or never rose above the level of sorcery and incantation. To define the relation between these two conceptions is extremely difficult, and it has been approached by different writers along two different lines of thought. Either the gods were developed

---

[1] E. B. Tylor, *Primitive Culture*, vol. ii. p. 202.

from the spiritual forces assumed by primitive man to be inherent in nature, and gradually differentiated from the less friendly powers embodied in the various demons, until they came to be regarded as the kinsmen and parents of their worshippers; or they were ancestral spirits, at once feared and trusted from their very origin by their kinsmen, whilst all the class of minor spirits and demons were but degenerate gods or the ancestral spirits of enemies. The former view is put forward by Professor Robertson Smith, in a chapter that deserves most careful study, but he admits that it is difficult to understand how the friendly powers of nature that haunted a district in which men lived and prospered, and were regarded as embodied in holy trees and springs, became identified with the tribal god of a community and the parent of a race.[1] There is no such difficulty in Mr. Herbert Spencer's theory that all religion arose from ancestor worship, or in Mr. Grant Allen's supplementary contention that trees and stones came to be regarded as sacred and to be honoured with sacrifices because they were originally associated with the ancestral grave, and were hence assumed to have become the haunts or embodiments of the ancestral spirit.[2] This latter view, however, does not seem to take sufficient account of the thousand spirits who, in the belief of primitive men, thronged the woods, the mountains, and the springs, and appeared in horrible animal or semi-human form. Probably the truth lies between the two theories, and the primitive worship of the tree had more than one root.

[1] *Op. cit.* Lecture III.
[2] The Attis of Catullus (London, 1892), Excursus II.

CHAPTER II

THE GOD AND THE TREE

WHEN we examine more closely the spiritual beings who have been thought to haunt or inhabit vegetation, we find that they fall more or less distinctly into two classes—into tree-gods on the one hand, and on the other into the various tree-demons, wood-spirits, dryads, elves, jinns, and fabulous monsters common to the mythology of all countries. There is, perhaps, no absolutely definite line of demarcation between the two classes, for primitive thought does not deal in sharp definitions. But the division, besides being convenient for our present purpose, is a vital one. For a god is an individual spirit who enters into stated relations with man, is mostly if not invariably regarded as akin to his worshippers, and is presumably their friend, ally, and protector. Whereas the demon is an independent and, as a rule, not individualised spirit, without human kinship, and for the most part unfriendly to man. The god is to be revered, approached and called upon by name; the demon, as a rule, to be dreaded and shunned. The present chapter will be devoted to the belief in the tree-inhabiting god.

The conception of an ubiquitous, unconditioned spirit is entirely foreign to primitive thought. All the gods of antiquity were subject to physical limitations. Those even of Greece and Rome were by no means independent of a material environment. There was always some holy place or sanctuary, some grove, tree, stone, or fountain, or later on some temple or image, wherein the god was assumed to dwell, and through which he had to be approached. To Moses Jehovah is "He that dwelt in the bush,"[1] and centuries later Cyrus, while admitting that the Lord of Israel had made him king of the whole world, yet speaks of Him as "the Lord that dwelleth in Jerusalem."[2] Very frequently, especially in early times, this home or haunt of the god was a tree; his ceremonial worship was conducted beneath its shadow, and the offerings of his worshippers were hung upon its branches, or placed at its foot, or upon a table by its side, and assumed thereby to have reached the god. Thus the sacred sycamores of Egypt were believed to be actually inhabited by Hāthor, Nûit, Selkit, Nit, or some other deity, and were worshipped and presented with offerings as such. The vignettes in the *Book of the Dead* demonstrate this belief unmistakably. They frequently depict the soul on its journey to the next world coming to one of these miraculous sycamores on the edge of the terrible desert before it, and receiving from the goddess of the tree a supply of bread, fruit, or water, the acceptance of which made it the guest of the deity and prevented it from retracing its steps without her express permission. "O, sycamore of the Goddess Nûit," begins one of the chapters in the *Book of the Dead*,

---

[1] Deuteronomy xxxiii. 16.   [2] 1 Esdras ii. 5.

"let there be given to me the water which is in thee." As a rule in the vignettes the bust of the goddess is represented as appearing from amidst the sheltering foliage, but sometimes only her arm is seen emerging from the leaves with a libation-bowl in the hand. The conception is illustrated still more clearly on an ancient sarcophagus in the Marseilles

FIG. 10.—The goddess Nüit in her sacred sycamore bestowing the bread and water of the next world.

(Maspero, *Dawn of Civilisation*.)

Museum, where the trunk from which the branches spread is represented as the actual body of the deity.[1]

As man's conception of the deity became more definitely anthropomorphic on the one hand and less local on the other, this primitive representation of the god in the tree underwent a change in two corresponding directions. In the one case an attempt was made to

[1] Maspero, *op. cit.* p. 84, note 1.

express more clearly the manlike form of the god; the tree was dressed or carved in human semblance, or a mask or statue of the god was hung upon or placed beside it. In the other case, as the god widened his territory or absorbed other local gods he

FIG. 11.—Sacred tree of Dionysus, with a statue of the god and offerings.
(Bötticher, Fig. 24.)

became associated with all trees of a certain class, and was assumed to dwell not in a particular tree, but in a particular kind of tree, which thenceforward became sacred to and symbolical of him. This latter idea received special development in the religions of Greece and Rome. But in the early history of both those countries cases occur in which a god was worshipped in an individual tree. At Dodona, which was perhaps the most ancient of all Greek sanctuaries, Zeus was approached as immanent in his sacred oak, and legendary afterthought explained the primitive ritual by relating that the first oak sprang from the blood of a Titan slain while invading the abode of the god, who thereupon chose it as his own peculiar tree. Again, in ancient Rome, according to Livy, Jupiter was originally worshipped in the form of a lofty oak-tree which grew upon the Capitol. The same was probably true of other gods at their first appearance. Amongst the Greeks, indeed, the tree was the earliest symbol or ἄγαλμα of the god, and as such is frequently represented on ancient vases, marble tablets, silver vessels, and wall-paintings. Indeed, the solitary tree standing in Attic fields and worshipped as the sacred habitation of a god was in all probability the earliest Greek temple, the forerunner of those marvellous edifices which have aroused the admiration of every subsequent age; whilst the elaborate worship of which those temples became the home was presumably based upon a ceremonial originally connected with the worship of the tree.

According to Mr. Farnell, the latest writer on the

FIG. 12.—Sacred pine of Silvanus, with a bust of the god, and votive gifts represented by a bale of merchandise and a Mercury's staff.
(Bötticher, Fig 18.)

subject, the chief gods of the Greeks were in their origin deities of vegetation, the special attributes which we associate with them being subsequent accretions. The pre-Hellenic Cronos gave his name to an Attic harvest-festival held in July, and his ancient emblem was the sickle.[1] Zeus, besides being the oak-god of Dodona, was worshipped in Attica as a god of agriculture and honoured with cereal offerings.[2] Artemis was not primarily a goddess of chastity, nor a moon-goddess, nor the twin-sister of Apollo, but an independent divinity, closely related to the wood-nymphs, and connected with water and with wild vegetation and forest beasts. She was worshipped in Arcadia as the goddess of the nut-tree and the cedar, and in Laconia as the goddess of the laurel and the myrtle. Her idol at Sparta was said to have been found in a willow brake, bound round with withies. At Teuthea in Achaea she was worshipped as the goddess of the woodland pasture, and at Cnidus as the nurturer of the hyacinth.[3] In the legend of the colonisation of Boiae she was represented as embodied in a hare which suddenly disappeared in a myrtle-tree.[4] But her character as a tree-goddess comes out still more clearly in the cult of the "hanging Artemis" at Kaphyae in Arcadia,[5] which no doubt grew out of the primitive custom of suspending a mask or image of the vegetation spirit to the sacred tree.

The association of Hera with tree-worship is less pronounced. She was said to have been born under a willow-tree at Samos, and her worship in that island was characterised by a yearly ceremony in which her priestess secreted her idol in a willow brake, where it

---

[1] Farnell, *op. cit.* vol. i. chap. iii. [4] *Ibid.* vol. ii. p. 432.
[2] *Ibid.* vol. i. p. 66. [5] Pausanias, 8, 23, 6.
[3] *Ibid.* vol. ii. p. 429.

was subsequently rediscovered and honoured with an oblation of cakes.[1] In Argos she was worshipped as the deity who gave the fruits of the earth, and as such was represented with a pomegranate in her hand. It is also worthy of note that the familiar symbol of a conventionalised tree between two griffins appears on the stephanos or coronet of the goddess on coins of Croton of the fourth century, and of certain South Italian cities, as well as on a colossal bust now at Venice, which, like the head on the coins, was presumably copied from the temple-image at Croton.[2]

Aphrodite was not a primitive Greek deity, but her connection with vegetative life is abundantly clear. She was, in fact, but a Hellenised variant of the great Oriental goddess, worshipped in different parts as Istar, Astarte, Cybele, etc., who was essentially a divinity of vegetation.[3]

This primitive connection of the gods of Greece with vegetative life was lost sight of in their later developments. Even at the date of the Homeric poems the more advanced of the Greeks had evidently arrived at "a highly developed structure of religious thought, showing us clear-cut personal divinities with ethical and spiritual attributes."[4] But the older and cruder ideas of the nature of the gods left a persistent trace in the ritual with which they were worshipped, as well as in the designs of the artists who reflected the popular traditions. Thus the ancient custom of burning incense before the tree, decking it with consecrated fillets, and honouring it with burnt offerings, survived long after the belief of which it was the natural development had decayed. A sculp-

---

[1] Farnell, *op. cit.* vol. i. p. 185.
[2] *Ibid.* vol. i. p. 212.
[3] *Ibid.* vol. ii. p. 644.
[4] *Ibid.* vol. i. p. 9.

ture preserved in the Berlin Museum represents the holy pine-tree of Pan adorned with wreaths and fillets. An image of Pan is near, and offerings are being brought to an altar placed beneath it. Again, Theocritus describes how at the consecration of Helen's plane-tree at Sparta, the choir of Lacedaemonian maidens hung consecrated wreaths of lotus flowers upon the tree, anointed it with costly spikenard, and attached to it the dedicatory placard : " Honour me, all ye that pass by, for I am Helen's tree."[1]

The practice of giving the tree a human semblance, by clothing it in garments or carving its stump in human form, was the natural result of this worship amongst an artistic race, groping its way towards a concrete expression of its ideas. It represented the crude strivings of a people who, in their attempts to create gods in their own image, eventually produced

FIG. 13.—Fruit-tree dressed as Dionysus.
(Bötticher, Fig. 44.)

an unsurpassable ideal of human grace and beauty. From the rudely carved tree-stump arose in due time the Hermes of Praxiteles. Bötticher reproduces several ancient designs in which the trunk of a tree is dressed as Dionysus. In one of these a mask is fastened at the top of the trunk in such a way that the branches appear to grow from the head of the god, and the trunk itself is clothed with a long

[1] Theocritus, *Idyll.* xviii. 48.

garment; a table, or altar, loaded with gifts, stands beside it.[1]

In other cases, probably where the worshipped tree had died, its trunk or branches were rudely carved into an image of the god, and either left *in situ*, or hewn down and placed near the temple or, later, in the very temple itself. Both Pausanias and Pliny state that the oldest images of the gods were made of wood, and several Latin authors refer to the custom of thus carving the branches of auspicious trees (*felicium arborum*) as prevalent in primitive times amongst the Greeks.[2] The ἄγαλμα or emblem of Aphrodite, dedicated by Pelops, was wrought out of a fresh verdant myrtle-tree. At Samos a board was the emblem of Hera; two wooden stocks joined together by a cross-piece was the sign of the twin-brethren at Sparta, and a wooden column encircled with ivy was consecrated to Dionysus at Thebes.[3]

It may be fairly assumed that in cases such as these the worshippers believed that the dead piece of wood retained some at least of the power originally attributed to the spirit dwelling in the living tree. Their idolatry was but a childish deduction from an ancient and deeply-rooted theology. The same may be said for the wood-cutter, derided in the Apocrypha, who, "taking a crooked piece of wood and full of knots, carveth it with the diligence of his idleness, and shapeth it by the skill of his indolence; then he giveth it the semblance of the image of a man, smearing it with vermilion and with paint colouring it red; and having made for it a chamber worthy of it, he setteth it in a wall, making it fast with iron."[4] Side by side

---

[1] Bötticher, *op. cit.* pp. 103, 229.
[2] *Ibid.* pp. 217, 220.
[3] Farnell, *op. cit.* vol. i. p. 14.
[4] Wisdom xiii. 11 (Revised Version).

with this foolish wood-cutter, who "for life beseecheth that which is dead," may be placed the Sicilian peasant whom Theocritus represents as offering sacrifice to a carved Pan. "When thou hast turned yonder lane, goatherd, where the oak-trees are, thou wilt find an image of fig-tree wood newly carven; three legged it is, the bark still covers it, and it is earless withal. A right holy precinct runs round it, and a ceaseless stream that falleth from the rocks on every side is green with laurels and myrtles and fragrant cypress. And all around the place that child of the grape, the vine, doth flourish with its tendrils, and the merles in spring with their sweet songs pour forth their woodnotes wild, and the brown nightingales reply with their complaints, pouring from their bills their honey sweet song."[1]

This crude worship of the god in the anthropomorphised tree lingered on amongst the peasantry side by side with the splendid temple ritual, even into days when the revelation of a Deity who filled all time and space, and was worshipped in temples not made with hands, was rapidly undermining the pagan worship of the cities. Maximus Tyrius, who lived in the second century A.D., and counted among his most diligent pupils the great Marcus Aurelius, relates how even in his day at the festival of Dionysus every peasant selected the most beautiful tree in his garden to convert it into an image of the god and to worship it.[2] And Apuleius, another writer of the same period, bears similar testimony. "It is the custom," he says, "of pious travellers, when their way passes a grove or holy place, that they offer up a prayer for the fulfilment of their wishes, offer gifts and remain there a

[1] Theocritus, *Epigram*. IV.   [2] Maximus Tyrius, viii. 1.

time; so I, when I set foot in that most sacred city, although in haste, must crave for a pardon, offer a prayer and moderate my haste. For never was traveller more justified in making a religious pause, when he perchance shall have come upon a flower-wreathed altar, a grotto covered with boughs, an oak decorated with many horns, or a beech-tree with skins

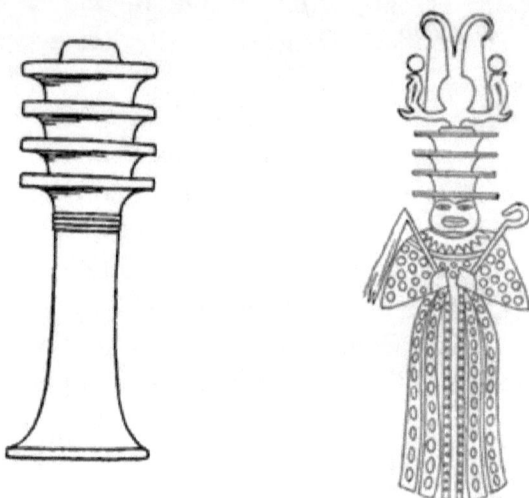

FIGS. 14, 15.—Forms of the Tât or Didû, the emblem of Osiris.
(Maspero, *op. cit.*)

hung to it, a little sacred hill fenced around, or a *tree trunk hewn as an image* (*truncus dolamine effigatus*)."[1]

This custom of carving a tree into the semblance of a god, and subsequently worshipping it as his sanctuary or symbol, was current in many parts of the world. The chief idol form of Osiris, the Didû or Tât, is believed by Maspero to have originated as a simple tree-trunk disbranched and planted in the ground.[2] Usually it is represented with a grotesque face, beneath

[1] Apuleius, *Florid.* i. 1.
[2] Maspero, *op. cit.* p. 84, note 3, and p. 130.

four superimposed capitals, with a necklace round its neck, a long robe hiding the base of the column in its folds, and the whole surmounted by the familiar Osirian emblems.

Again, it is said to have been a practice amongst the Druids, when an oak died to strip off its bark and shape it into a pillar, pyramid, or cross, and continue to worship it as an emblem of the god.[1] The cross especially was a favourite form, and any oak with two principal branches forming a cross with the main stem was consecrated by a sacred inscription, and from that time forward regarded with particular reverence.

The same custom prevailed in India. In the seventeenth century there existed near Surat a sacred banian-tree, supposed to be 3000 years old, which the Hindus would never cut or touch with steel for fear of offending the god concealed in its foliage. They made pilgrimages to it and honoured it with religious ceremonies. On its trunk at a little distance from the ground a head had been roughly carved, painted in gay colours, and furnished with gold and silver eyes. This simulacrum was constantly adorned with fresh foliage and flowers, the withered leaves which they replaced being distributed amongst the pilgrims as pious souvenirs.[2]

It was predominantly, though by no means exclusively, a Greek development to associate a particular god with a particular variety of tree. The oak, excelling all others in majestic strength and inherent vigour, became the emblem and embodiment of Zeus. The connection arose in all probability from the primitive worship of the Pelasgic Zeus in the oak

---

[1] Folkard, *op. cit.* p. 467.
[2] De Gubernatis, *Mythologie des Plantes*, vol. ii. p. 26 *et seq.*

grove of Dodona, but in classical times it was accepted throughout Greece. On coins and in other works of art the god is frequently represented as crowned with oak leaves, or as standing or sitting beside an oak-tree.[1] To have partaken of the acorns of Zeus was a vernacular expression for having acquired wisdom and knowledge. This especial sanctity of the oak as the tree of the father of the gods passed into Italy, and Virgil speaks of it as—

> Jove's own tree
> That holds the world in awful sovereignty.

Fig. 16.—Apollo on his sacred tripod, a laurel branch in his hand.

(From a coin, probably of Delphi.)

More sacred even than the oak to Zeus was the laurel to Apollo. No sanctuary of his was complete without it; none could be founded where the soil was unfavourable to its growth. No worshipper could share in his rites who had not a crown of laurel on his head or a branch in his hand. As endowed with the power of the god, who was at once the prophet, poet, redeemer, and protector of his people, the laurel assumed an important and many-sided rôle in ceremonial symbolism.[2] The staff of laurel in the hand of the reciting poet was assumed to assist his inspiration, in the hand of the prophet or diviner to help him to see hidden things. Thus the use of the laurel played an essential part in the oracular ceremonial of Delphi. Everywhere, in short, the bearing of the laurel bough was the surest way to the god's protection and favour. The conception was slow to die. Clement, writing about 200 A.D., still finds the warning necessary that

---

[1] Farnell, *op. cit.* vol. i. pp. 108-110.   [2] Bötticher, *op. cit.* p. 345.

"one must not hope to obtain reconciliation with God by means of laurel branches adorned with red and white ribbons."[1]

By an easy transition the laurel became sacred also to Aesculapius. As the source at once of a valuable remedy and a deadly poison, it was held in high esteem by Greek physicians. It was popularly believed that spirits could be cast out by its means, and it was usual to affix a laurel bough over the doorway in cases of serious illness, in order to avert death and keep evil spirits at bay.[2]

The ceremonial use of the laurel passed from Greece into Italy. When the Sibylline books were consulted at Rome, the laurel of prophecy always adorned the chair of the priest.[3] Victors were crowned with laurel, and in Roman triumphs the soldiers decked their spears and helmets with its leaves.

The tree of Aphrodite was the myrtle.[4] It was held to have the power both of creating and of perpetuating love, and hence from the earliest times was used in marriage ceremonies. In the Eleusinian mysteries the initiates crowned themselves with the oak leaves of Zeus and the myrtle of Aphrodite. The Graces, her attendants, were represented as wearing myrtle chaplets, and her worshippers crowned themselves with myrtle sprays. At Rome Venus was worshipped under the name of Myrtea in her temple at the foot of the Aventine. The apple-tree held a subsidiary but yet important place in the cult of Aphrodite. Its fruit was regarded as an appropriate offering to her and, according to Theocritus, played

---

[1] Clemens Alex., *Protrepticus*, cap. 1, sect. 10.
[2] Folkard, *op. cit.* p. 407.
[3] Bötticher, *op. cit.* p. 351.
[4] *Ibid.* p. 445.

its part in love games.¹ The apples of Atalanta had no doubt a symbolical significance.

Athena also had her special tree. According to mythology she sprang fully armed from the head of Zeus, but research into the origins of the gods makes it much more probable that her true pedigree was from the olive, which grew wild upon the Athenian Acropolis, the chief seat of her worship. Mr. M'Lennan even inclined to regard the olive as originally the totem of the Athenians.² At any rate their connection with that tree dates from an ancient time. "The produce of the olive-tree had an almost religious value for the men of Attica, and the physical side of Greek civilisation much depended on it."³ From the era of Pericles onwards the coins of Athens were stamped with the olive-branch, amongst other usual accompaniments of the tutelary goddess. Every sanctuary and temple of Athena had its sacred olive-tree, which was regarded as the symbol of the divine peace and protection. Naturally a legend arose to explain the connection. Athena and Poseidon, being at variance as to which of them should name the newly-founded city of Athens, referred the question to the gods, who in general assembly decreed the privilege to that claimant who should give the most

FIG. 17.—Coin of Athens, of the age of Pericles or earlier, showing olive spray.

FIG. 18.—Coin of Athens, third century B.C.

---

¹ Theocritus, *Idyll.* vi. 7.   ² *Fortnightly Review*, February 1870.
³ Farnell, *op. cit.* vol. i. p. 292.

useful present to the inhabitants of earth. Poseidon struck the ground with his trident and a horse sprang forth. But Athena "revealed the spray of the gray-green olive, a divine crown and glory for bright Athens."[1] And the gods decided that the olive, as the emblem of peace, was a higher gift to man than the horse, which was the symbol of war. So Athena named the city after herself and became its protectress. This myth, which, according to Mr. Farnell, is one of the very few creation-myths in Greek folk-lore, was a favourite subject in art, and is frequently represented on late Attic coins.[2]

Other gods had their sacred trees: Dionysus, the vine; Dis and Persephone, the poplar, which was supposed to grow on the banks of Acheron. The cypress, called by Greeks and Romans alike the "mournful tree," was also sacred to the rulers of the underworld, and to their associates, the Fates and Furies. As such it was customary to plant it by the grave, and, in the event of a death, to place it either before the house or in the vestibule, in order to warn those about to perform a sacred rite against entering a place polluted by a dead body.[3]

In regard to the number of trees which they held sacred the Semitic nations rivalled the Greeks. They venerated "the pines and cedars of Lebanon, the evergreen oaks of the Palestinian hills, the tamarisks of the Syrian jungles, the acacias of the Arabian wadies," besides such cultivated trees as the palm, the olive, and the vine. But there is no clear evidence to prove that they ever coupled a particular species of tree with a particular god. In Phoenicia the cypress

---

[1] Euripides, *Troades*, 795.
[2] Farnell, *op. cit.* vol. i. p. 325.
[3] Pliny, xvi. 60; Servius ad Virgil. *Aen.* iv. 507.

was sacred to Astarte, but it was equally connected with the god Melcarth, who was believed to have planted the cypress-trees at Daphne. "If a tree belonged to a particular deity, it was not because it was of a particular species, but because it was the natural wood of the place where the god was worshipped."[1] It is true that the Chaldaeans regarded the cedar as the special tree of the god Ea, but the association was probably borrowed, like the god himself, from the non-Semitic Accadians, while the connection of the Nabataean god, Dusares, with the vine may be traced to Hellenic influence.

Outside the Semitic area individual gods are often found, as in Greece, linked with particular kinds of trees. In Persia the cypress was the sacred tree of the god Mithra, while in Egypt the acacia was intimately associated with Osiris. On an ancient sarcophagus an acacia is represented with the device, "Osiris shoots up."[2] And in mortuary pictures the god is sometimes represented as a mummy covered with a tree or with growing plants. In both cases the idea of life arising out of death is probably implied.

In India each Buddha was associated with his own bodhi-tree or tree of wisdom. The trumpet-flower, the sâl-tree, the acacia, the pippala, and the banian all belonged to different Buddhas, and are so depicted on the Stûpa of Bharhut. Here in the case of the earliest of the Buddhas whose bodhi-tree has been found, the Buddha Vipasin, the particular tree represented is the *pâtali* or trumpet-flower. In front of it is placed "a throne or bodhi-manda, before which two people are kneeling, whilst a

---

[1] Robertson Smith, *op. cit.* p. 175.
[2] Tiele, *Religion de l'Égypte*, etc. p. 83.

crowd of others with joined hands are standing on each side of the tree."[1] The Buddha Gautama's tree was the pippala or *Ficus religiosa*, which is much more elaborately treated at Bharhut than any other bodhi-tree. In the sculpture representing its adoration, "the trunk is entirely surrounded by an open pillared building with an upper story, ornamented with niches containing umbrellas. Two umbrellas are placed in the top of the tree, and numerous streamers are hanging from the branches. In the two upper corners are flying figures with wings, bringing offerings of garlands. On each side there is a male figure raising a garland in his right hand and holding the tip of his tongue with the thumb and forefinger of his left. In the lower story of the building is a throne in front of a tree. Two figures, male and female, are kneeling before the throne, while a female figure is standing to the left, and a Nâga Raja with his hands crossed on his breast to the right. This figure is distinguished by a triple serpent crest. To the extreme right there is an isolated pillar surmounted by an elephant holding

FIG. 19.—The Bodhi-tree of Kanaka Muni (*Ficus glomerata*).

(*The Stûpa of Bharhut*, by Major-General Cunningham, Plate XXIV. 4.)

---

[1] A. Cunningham, *The Stûpa of Bharhut* (London, 1879), p. 113.

out a garland in his trunk. On the domed roof of the building is inscribed, 'The Bodhi-Tree of the Buddha Sâkya Muni.'"[1] In another sculpture elephants old and young are paying their devotions to a banian-tree, while others are bringing garlands to hang on its

FIG. 20.—Wild elephants paying their devotions to the sacred banian of Kâsyapa Buddha.

(*The Stûpa of Bharhut*, Plate xv.)

branches. The important bearing of these sculptures on the history of tree-worship is obvious.

It may be noted in passing that neither in the many sculptured scenes at Bharhut and Buddha Gaya, all of which are contemporary with Asoka (*circa* 250 B.C.), nor even in the much later sculptures of Sanchi dating from the end of the first century A.D.

---

[1] A. Cunningham, *op. cit.* p. 114.

is there any representation of Buddha, the sole objects of reverence being stûpas (representations of the tombs of holy men), wheels, or trees. At a later date the tree appears to have lost its organic connection with the venerated personage, and to have preserved only a ceremonial and symbolic significance, for the Bo-tree, under which truth gradually unfolded itself to the meditating Gautama, is regarded as sacred by Buddhists in much the same way as the cross is by Christians.

There can be no doubt, however, that in the earliest forms of worship current in India, the alliance between the plant world and the divine essence was extremely intimate. The great creative god Brahma, who, by the light of his countenance, dispelled the primeval gloom, and by his divine influence evoked the earth from the primeval ocean, is represented in Hindu theology as having emanated from a golden lotus which had been quickened into life when the spirit of Om moved over the face of the waters. Again, in Brahminical worship the very essence of the deity is supposed to descend into his tree. The tulasi or holy basil of India is believed by the Hindus to be pervaded by the divinity of Vishnu and of his wife Lakshmi, and hence is venerated as a god. It opens the gates of heaven to the pious worshipper, and those who uproot it will be punished by Vishnu in time and eternity.[1]

In fact, in the twilight of religion, wherever we turn, the same idea of a tree-inhabiting god prevails. In the mythology of Northern Europe the grove of Upsala, the most sacred spot in all the Scandinavian peninsula, was the home of Woden, the god who, after

[1] Folkard, *op. cit.* p. 245.

hanging for nine nights on the gallows-tree, descended to the underworld and brought back the prize of wisdom in the form of nine rune songs.[1] In the Middle Ages, according to the rule by which the gods of one age become the demons of the next, Woden was converted into Satan, his grove became the Brocken, and the Valkyrie degenerated into witches. Taara, the supreme god of the Finns and Esthonians, was associated with the oak, and the same is true of the Norse god, Balder, at whose death, we are told, men, animals, and plants wept. The principal god of the ancient Prussians was supposed to dwell by preference in the great oak at Romove,[2] before which a hierarchy of priests kept up a continual fire of oak-logs. The oak was veiled from view, like the pictures in a modern continental church, and only shown from time to time to its worshippers. The grove where it stood was so sacred that only the consecrated were allowed to enter, and no branch in it might be injured.[3]

FIG. 21.—Sacred sycamore, with offerings.

(Maspero, *op. cit.*)

If proof were needed of the reverence with which the tree was regarded in ancient times and of its hold upon the reverence of the people, as being the dwelling-place of the god, it could be found alone in the number

---

[1] C. F. Keary, *The Vikings of Western Christendom* (London, 1891), pp. 36, 52, 53.
[2] Frazer, *op. cit.* vol. i. p. 64.
[3] J. Grimm, *op. cit.* vol. i. p. 369.

of the gifts, which, by the evidence of ancient literature and art, it was the practice to hang upon its branches or place about its trunk. In Arabia there was a tree, identified by Robertson Smith with the sacred acacia of Nakhla, the dwelling-place of the goddess Al-'Ozza, on which the people of Mecca at an annual pilgrimage hung weapons, garments, ostrich eggs, and other offerings.[1] It is spoken of in the traditions of Mahomet by the vague name of a *dhát anwát*, or "tree to hang things on." Another Arabian tree, the sacred date-palm at Nejrân, was also adored at an annual feast, and hung with fine clothes and women's ornaments.[2] In Egypt, offerings of figs, grapes, cucumbers, etc. were habitually made to the deities inhabiting the sycamores.

FIG. 22.—Sacred tree of Artemis, hung with weapons of the chase.

(Bötticher, Fig. 9.)

A similar custom was well known in Greece, as is proved by the many vases and sculptured tablets in

---

[1] Robertson Smith, *op. cit.* p. 169.
[2] Sir W. Ouseley, *Travels*, vol. i. p. 369.

which the tree is shown hung with consecrated fillets and offerings, while the altar beneath groans with gifts. Statius, writing in the second century B.C., describes a widely celebrated tree, amongst many others similarly laden, as being covered with bows and arrows, heads of boars, skins of lions, and huge horns, which had been dedicated to it as trophies of the chase.[1] Conquerors, returning from battle, would hang their weapons on the sacred tree with a dedication to the all-powerful Zeus. The arms thus dedicated were respected even by the enemy.

This custom of making offerings to the tree is no doubt of great antiquity. In the legend of the Golden Fleece, Phryxus, having been carried by the fabled ram across the Hellespont, sacrificed it to Ares, and hung its priceless fleece on the boughs of a sacred beech-tree,[2] whence it was subsequently recovered by Jason. Such dedication at the shrines of the gods of something that had been of service and still had value to the worshipper, was very common in Greek and Roman worship, and in many cases the tree was the recipient of the gift.[3] The rich brought their jewels, the poor their homely tools and utensils. The fisherman dedicated his nets in gratitude for an exceptional catch. The shepherd offered his flute as a welcome gift to Pan. Some of the dedicatory inscriptions preserve for us the pathos of the gift. "Daphnis, the flute-player, bowed with shaking age, has here dedicated his shepherd's staff, too heavy for his weak hand, to meadow-loving Pan."[4] Lais, grown old, hangs her too truthful mirror on the sacred tree of Aphrodite. "Take it, O lovely Cytherea; to thee

---

[1] Statius, *Theb.* ix. 585.
[2] Apollon. Rhod. *Argonaut.* 2.
[3] Cf. Ovid, *Metamorphoses*, viii. 743.
[4] Bötticher, *op. cit.* p. 79.

alone is undying beauty given."[1] In the same way Bacchic revellers, their frenzy past, brought to the tree the cymbals, robes, and perfumed tresses they had used.[2]

There is further evidence of the sanctity of the tree in the important function given to branches and wreaths in religious ceremonies, a custom which can find logical explanation only in a precedent tree-worship deeply rooted in the popular mind. In the service of the gods of Greece and Rome the wreath was indispensable. An uncrowned worshipper was in the position of the man in the parable who had no wedding garment. And the wreath must have been taken from the particular tree of the god worshipped, so that the worshipper might be placed in closest communion with the deity, and remain inviolate from molestation while thus clothed with the divine protection.[3]

The carrying of the sacred branch in solemn procession formed the essential feature in some of the most important religious festivals of Greece. At the Daphnephoria, held every nine years at Thebes in Boeotia in honour of Apollo, the chief post in the procession was held by the Daphnephorus, or laurel-bearer, a boy chosen for his strength and beauty. He was followed to the temple of the god by a chorus of maidens, also bearing branches and chanting a processional hymn, and was regarded for the occasion as the priest of Apollo, who himself bore amongst his many other appellations that of Daphnephorus, because he had brought the laurel to Delphi and planted it there.[4]

[1] Orelli, No. 1266.
[2] Bötticher, *op. cit.* p. 88.
[3] *Ibid.* chap. xxi.
[4] *Ibid.* p. 385.

At the Pyanepsia and the Thargelia, two important Athenian festivals, the *Eiresione*, a harvest wreath of olive or laurel bound round with red and white wool, and hung with the choicest first-fruits, was borne about by singing boys, while offerings were made to the gods.¹ A vine branch with the grapes upon it gave its name to another Athenian festival, the Oschophoria, or grape carrying, held in honour of Dionysus. A race between chosen youths formed one of the events of the festival, the competitors running from the temple of Dionysus to that of Athena, with boughs in their hands.²

Apart, however, from these important festivals, the use of wreaths or branches was a familiar incident in the daily life of the Greeks, bearing with it always a sort of religious significance. The bringer of good news was rewarded with a wreath; the guests at a feast were crowned with flowers. No gift to the gods was complete without its floral accompaniment, and their statues were often hidden under the wreaths brought thither as the most acceptable offering.

It can scarcely be doubted that this lavish employment of blossom and leaf as the expression of a religious emotion originally sprang from reverence for the tree as the favourite home of a god. The Greeks, with their instinctive love for all things beautiful, naturally pushed this graceful custom further than other races. But the ceremonial use of branches and flowers was common throughout the East. The Chaldaean sacred texts mention the use of "green branches" in religious ceremonies.³ At the Feast of Tabernacles the Israelites were enjoined to "take the boughs of goodly trees,

---

[1] Bötticher, chap. xxv.   [2] *Ibid.* p. 398.
[3] Sayce, *op. cit.* pp. 536, 539.

branches of palm-trees, and the boughs of thick trees and willows of the brook, and rejoice before the Lord."[1] The Apocrypha mentions the "festal olive boughs of the Temple."[2] In Persia and Armenia it was customary to bear a branch when approaching the god. In Egypt Isis was worshipped with sprays of absinthe, palm-branches were carried in funeral processions, and lotus wreaths usually worn at feasts, whilst in the Assyrian sculptures illustrious persons are frequently represented holding a flower.[3]

However little benefit the votaries of trees and images derived from their observances, apart from the subjective strength and solace that flow from every act of worship, there was at least one tangible service their gods could render them—the right of sanctuary and asylum. For the sacred tree, sharing as it did in the protective power of the indwelling deity, offered an inviolable refuge to the persecuted and the god's forgiveness to the sinner who implored it. To have touched it was regarded amongst the Greeks as equivalent to having touched an altar or statue of the god. A branch of it, entwined with the consecrated fillet, assured its bearer from persecution. Hence a possible explanation of the legend of the young Dionysus standing secure amongst the branches of the sacred tree whilst the flames raged around him.

Frequent references occur in the Classics to tree-sanctuaries. The Amazons, defeated by Hercules, found a safe asylum beneath the holy tree at Ephesus, which was worshipped both as the symbol and temple of Artemis, before her statue was set up in the tree or her temple built around it.[4] Herodotus relates how

---

[1] Leviticus xxiii. 40.
[2] 2 Maccabees xiv. 4.
[3] Bötticher, *op. cit.* pp. 321, 322.
[4] Pausanias, vii. 2, 4.

Cleomenes, having burnt the sacred grove of Argos,

FIG. 23.—Sacred laurel of Apollo at Delphi, adorned with fillets and votive tablets; beneath it the god appearing to protect Orestes.

(From a vase-painting, Bötticher, Fig. 2.)

together with the five thousand conquered Argives who had taken refuge there, was visited by the gods

with madness for his act of sacrilege.[1] Orestes, in his
flight from the Furies, is represented on a Greek vase
as seeking refuge beneath Apollo's laurel.[2] The god
appears out of the tree to succour him and scare away
his pursuers. The cypress grove on the Acropolis at
Phlius in Peloponnesus was another instance. Fugitives
from justice on reaching it became inviolable, and
escaped prisoners hung upon its trees the chains for
which they had no further use,[3] just as the modern
cripple, whose limbs have been freed from the prison
of his palsy, dedicates his crutches to "our Lady of
Lourdes."

[1] Herodotus, vi. 75.   [2] Bötticher, *op. cit.* p. 35.
[3] Pausanias, ii. 13, 3.

CHAPTER III

WOOD-DEMONS AND TREE-SPIRITS

In nearly all parts of the world, as at nearly all periods of history, we find evidences of a belief in the existence of wood-spirits and tree-spirits, which, however they may differ in outward form, are strangely similar in their general characteristics. It cannot be asserted of *all* these beings that they were regarded as the actual spirits of individual trees, connected with them as closely as a man's soul is with his body, but it is emphatically true of some of them. To the class of wood-spirits as a whole belong certain at least of the *jinni* of Arabia, the woodland spirits of Greek and Roman mythology, and the wild men and elves of European folk-lore, besides the tree-inhabiting spirits of various uncivilised races. Though not always sharply demarcated from the gods, they differ from them, as a rule, in being regarded and spoken of generically, and in not having stated relations with man. Their alliances are rather with trees, plants, and animals, whose growth and prosperity are often believed to be under their protection, and their presence is often assumed to be expressed in natural phenomena, in the mysterious sounds of the woods, and in the fury of the storm. To man they are frequently unfriendly, and numerous observances, still practised in uncivilised parts, have arisen from the belief that it was necessary to propitiate their favour.

Broadly speaking, their friendliness to man is directly proportionate to their human semblance, and this in its turn would seem to depend on the extent to which man has been able to conquer the dangers of the regions where they dwell. The farther back they are traced the more animal-like and inhuman their appearance. They preceded the gods and outlasted them, flourishing in times when these were still animal and totemistic, and retaining their animal characteristics long after the gods had become anthropomorphic. To the peasant mind there was, perhaps, no very clear distinction between the two classes, and the line between them has never been an unpassable one, for demons may develop into gods, just as gods may degenerate into demons. It is not claimed that all, or indeed most demons were tree-spirits in their origin, but a large class of them at any rate were closely associated with vegetable life and the phenomena that foster or threaten it.

Chaldaean mythology recognised, side by side with gods emphatically human, a class of fabulous monsters who were essentially demons and inferior spirits. There is not much evidence to couple these monsters with trees, but in one of the Babylonian hymns the aid of the gods is invoked against a terrible demon who "makes all creatures hurry in fear," and of whom it is stated that "his hand is the storm-demon, his eye is filled with the shadow of the forest, the sole of his foot is the lullub-tree."[1]

In the case of the *jinni* of Arabia the connection

---

[1] Sayce, *op. cit.* p. 493.

with trees is more clearly demonstrable. They were regarded as hairy monsters, more like beasts than men, haunting dense, untrodden thickets and endowed with the power of assuming various shapes. Such an uncouth and alarming presentment may well have arisen from their presumed association with places, which, as the natural lairs of dangerous animals, were perilous to man, but "the association of certain kinds of *jinni* with trees must in many cases be regarded as primary, the trees themselves being conceived as animated demoniac beings."[1] They have apparently had a longer career than most demons of the class, for their existence is still firmly believed in by certain Będouins, who asseverate that they have actually seen them. Mr. Theodore Bent found the same superstitious dread of the *jinni* both in the Hadramaut and in Dhofar. They are described as semi-divine spirits, who live by rocks near the streams, under trees, or in the lakes. Mr. Bent could not induce the Bedouins of his escort to gather a certain water-plant for fear of offending the *jinn* of the lake. In fact in the Gara Mountains the fear of the *jinni*, and the skill of certain magicians in keeping them friendly, appear to constitute the only tangible forms of religion.[2]

Under the word sĕīrīm, hairy monsters, E.V. "satyrs" and "devils," the Bible makes occasional mention of mythical creatures who were presumably related to the Arabian *jinni*.[3] They are represented as frequenting waste-places, forsaken by man and given over to nettles and brambles. In one passage the word is used of the heathen gods of Canaan,[4] whose close association with trees has already been noticed.

[1] Robertson Smith, *op. cit.* p. 125.
[2] *Nineteenth Century*, October 1895, p. 607.
[3] Isaiah xiii. 21 ; xxxiv. 14.
[4] Leviticus xvii. 7.

The fantastic monsters of the Egyptian desert, thought to appear only at the moment when the minor functions assigned to them had to be performed, and at other times to conceal themselves in inanimate objects, are represented as sometimes dwelling in trees or in stakes planted in the ground.[1] Their assumed complete incorporation in such objects is proved by the expressive term used by the Egyptians—the objects "ate them up." Their existence and their unfriendliness to man were firmly believed in. The shepherd feared them for his flock, the hunter for himself. Similar beasts roamed through the Egyptian Hades and threatened the wayfaring spirits of the dead.

These fragmentary evidences are important as casting a side-light on the parallel superstitions of the Aryan races, amongst which, as we shall see, the belief in wood-demons and tree-spirits was almost universal.

In Greek and Roman mythology there is a whole gallery of wild creatures inhabiting the mountains and woods, and more or less closely associated with vegetable life—centaurs and cyclops, Pans and satyrs, fauns and silvani, nymphs and dryads. Mannhardt has diligently compared these mythical beings with the wild people and wood-spirits of European folk-lore, and has clearly demonstrated a remarkable relationship.[2] In their evolution they present a distinctly progressive humanisation. The earliest of them, the centaurs and cyclops, remind us of the fabulous monsters of Semitic legend, and their contests with, and eventual disappearance before the higher powers seem paralleled in the similar conflict between the gods and demons of Chaldaea. Mannhardt adduces many arguments to prove that the centaurs first originated as

---
[1] Maspero, *op. cit.* pp. 83, 84.   [2] Mannhardt II. chap. ii.

local wood and mountain spirits. Their earliest haunt was the thickly wooded Pelion; one of them is represented as the son of the dryad Philyra or the linden; another as the son of Melia or the ash. Their weapons were uprooted trees. Like the European wild men of the woods they were covered with long shaggy hair. Chiron, the most friendly of them, was skilled in the use of simples and in the hidden powers of nature. Lastly, their presence was assumed in the whirlwind and other violent atmospheric phenomena. All these features class the archaic centaurs with the undoubted wood-spirits of a later mythology. The same is probably true of the cyclops, whose characteristics—their single eye, their use of uprooted trees for weapons, and their connection with sheep and goats—may be paralleled amongst the legendary wood-spirits of modern Europe.

In later times the place of the extinct centaurs and cyclops was taken by a tribe, half men half goats, known as Pan, satyrs, and sileni, who originally were in all probability local wood-spirits, Pan proceeding from Arcadia, the satyrs from Argos, the sileni from Phrygia. In the case of Pan we seem to see a class of doubtfully amicable wood-spirits developing into a more or less benevolent god. The Greek poets of the Periclean age speak of a whole tribe of wood-demons known as Panes or Panisci, from which eventually an individual, "the Great Pan," seems to have emerged. The son of a nymph, Pan is called in the Classics "god of the wood," "companion of kids," "goatherd." He is represented with horns and goat's legs, standing beside a sacred oak or pine, a fir-wreath on his head, and a branch in his hand. He leads the revels of the satyrs, pipes and dances amongst the wood-nymphs under the trees, and woos a pine-tree personified as Pithys. Like other wood-spirits he protects the herds, and, as befits a demon on the way to apotheosis, is for the most part friendly to man. But he never, apparently, quite lost his original character, for he is sometimes classed with incubi and spirits who cause evil dreams.

The satyr was a degraded, or rather unhumanised Pan, more sensual and malicious in character, coarser in feature, and more bestial in form. Hesiod calls the satyrs "a useless and crafty tribe." They were originally wood-demons, and men represented as satyrs took part in the festivals of Dionysus, the chief of vegetation spirits. Silenus, like Pan, the individualised head of a class, was also closely associated with Dionysus. The sileni, in fact, were but Phrygian variants of the satyrs, and are represented in the Homeric hymn to Aphrodite as consorting with the hamadryads. In Art they appear clothed in goat-skins. It may be added that the modern Greek peasant still believes in malicious goat-footed demons who inhabit the mountains.[1]

In Roman mythology the fauns and silvani played the same part as Pan and the satyrs in Greece, and the same confusion existed as to whether they were individual or generic. The fauns seldom appeared to mortal sight, but their presence was made known in the weird noises and the ghostly appearances of the dark forest. When seen they had horns and goat's feet, though in a later rendering they are more human in appearance. They guarded the flocks pasturing in the woods and, like other wood-spirits, also protected the cornfield. Silvanus and the silvani, as their name

---

[1] Mannhardt II. p. 139.

denotes, were tree-spirits even more emphatically than the fauns. According to Virgil the oldest inhabitants of Latium allotted to Silvanus a sacred grove and a special festival;[1] in later times he was universally regarded as the patron of the garden and field. At harvest time an offering of milk was poured over the roots of his sacred tree. In Art, Silvanus is represented as covered with hair (*horridus*) and standing under, or growing out of a garlanded tree, a crown of pine sprays on his head, a large pine bough in one hand and a sickle in the other. An inscription speaks of him as half enclosed in a sacred ash (*sacrâ semiclusus fraxino*). Another account associates the silvani with the fig-tree, and states that they were called by some *fauni ficarii*. Both fauns and silvani had an evil reputation for their supposed propensity to assault women, to carry off children, and to disturb the dreams of sleepers. The peasants of North Italy and Sicily still believe in wood-spirits, *gente selvatica*, closely resembling the old silvani. A Sicilian incantation is addressed to the spirit of the fig-tree and the devils of the nut-trees.[2]

Taking the sum of their characteristics, Mannhardt is doubtless right in classing these legendary beings with the wood-spirits met with in the folk-lore of Northern Europe.

It is, however, in the female counterparts of these woodland creatures that the idea of an actual tree-soul is most clearly exemplified. The most striking instance is the familiar one of the hamadryads, the deep-bosomed nymphs of wooded Ida, to whose care Aphrodite entrusted the infant Aeneas, and whose very name expresses their intimate connection with

---

[1] *Aeneid*, viii. 601.   [2] Mannhardt II. p. 31.

their trees. To quote the Homeric hymn to Aphrodite, which was probably written under Phrygian influence, " They belong neither to the mortals nor to the immortals: they live long, indeed, enjoying immortal food, and with the immortals they join in the lordly dance. The sileni mate with them, and Hermes, too, in the privy recesses of delightful grottoes. With them, when they were born, upon the mountains lofty pines and oaks sprang forth from the earth that gives food to man. Yet when at last the fate of death overtakes them, first the beautiful trees wither upon the earth, the bark dies around them, their branches fall away, and therewith the souls of the nymphs leave the light of the sun."[1]

Pindar, who would appear to have first given them the name of hamadryads, speaks of them as having the same length of life as a tree.[2]

But the case of the hamadryads is by no means an isolated example of the Greek belief in spirits whose life was bound up with the life of the tree. In the Homeric hymn to Ceres the nymphs rejoice when the oaks are in leaf, and weep when their branches become bare.[3] Elsewhere a nymph is depicted imploring that the oak wherein she dwelt should not be hewn down, and as bringing vengeance on him who ignored her entreaty.[4] It was not only the oak and the pine that might be inhabited by a spirit. Amongst the names of nymphs that have come down to us is Philyra (the linden), Daphne (the laurel), Rhoea (the pomegranate), and Helike (the willow). In later times an attempt was made in some cases to explain the connec-

---

[1] Hymn. Homer. Aphrod. 259-273.
[2] Plutarch, *De Defect. Orac.* 11.
[3] Hymn. in Cererem. 41.
[4] Apollonius Rhod., *Argonaut.* i. 471 *et seq.*

tion by metamorphosis, a living nymph being supposed to have been converted into a tree, but it is extremely probable that this was an inversion of the primitive nexus.

There are many instances closely parallel to these classical myths in mediaeval and modern legend. The story of Alexander and the flower-maidens, for instance, which was a favourite with the troubadours, and was subsequently popularised by Lamprecht, and later by Uhland, was presumably founded on a legend current in ancient Greece. The story goes that in a certain wood, when spring came, numbers of enormous flower buds appeared out of the ground, from each of which, as it opened, there leapt forth a beautiful maiden. Their robes were a part of their growth, and in colour they were just like their flowers, red and white. They played and danced in the shade, and their singing rivalled the birds'. All past heartaches were wiped away, and a life of joy and abundance seemed to open to him who saw them. But it was death for a maiden to leave her shady retreat and encounter the scorching sun. When summer was past, and the flowers withered and the birds were silent, the beautiful creatures died. Alexander and his knights, coming upon this magical wood, mated with the flower-maidens, and for more than three months lived in perfect happiness, till one by one the flowers faded, one by one the nymphs died, and the king and his companions had sorrowfully to resume their travels.[1]

Legends of this sort no doubt provided Lucian with the motive for that "true history" of his, wherein he tells of the wonderful vines growing on the far side of a certain river that ran wine instead of water.

[1] Mannhardt II. p. 1.

These vines below had a very thick stem, but above bore maidens' bodies of perfect form. Bunches of grapes grew from their finger-tips, and vine leaves and grapes formed their hair. They gave the travellers a friendly greeting, and bade them welcome, most speaking Greek, others Lydian or Indian. Whoever accepted their kisses felt a sudden drunken bewilderment. They shrieked aloud with pain when one attempted to pluck their grapes. Two of the travellers who surrendered themselves to their embraces could not get free again, but took root and budded forth vine leaves.[1]

The above, of course, was intended as a literary parody, but stories, not a whit less wonderful, are found in the folk-lore of many modern countries, and are no doubt recited and received in good faith. There is a modern Greek legend, for instance, of a childless wife, to whom Heaven, in answer to her prayer for children, sent a golden laurel berry. Despising the gift she threw it away. From it there grew a laurel-tree with golden sprays. A prince, following the chase, was so struck by its beauty that he ordered his dinner to be prepared beneath it. In the absence of the cook the tree opened and a fair maiden stepped forth, and after strewing a handful of salt over his food, withdrew to the tree, which immediately reinclosed her. The following day the prince again found his dinner spoilt, and on the third day he determined to keep watch. The maid came forth and was captured by the prince before she could regain her tree. After a time she escaped, and coming back to the tree called upon it to open and receive her. But it remained closed, and she was obliged to return to her prince, with whom,

[1] Lucian, *Verae Historiae*, lib. 1.

after various mischances, she lived happily for ever after.[1]

The Czekhs have a similar story of a nymph who roamed the forest by day, but at night invariably returned to her willow. She married a mortal and bore him a child. One day the willow was cut down and the nymph died. A cradle fashioned out of its wood had the power of lulling her child to sleep, and when he grew up he was able to hold converse with his mother by means of a pipe formed from the twigs which grew about the stump.[2]

That the soul of the nymph was thought actually to inhabit the tree is further proved by the belief current both in ancient and modern myth, that blood would flow when the tree was injured. It was firmly held in primitive times that the blood was the very life, the soul of an animal, and hence in primitive ritual it was the blood of the sacrifice that was offered to the god. It is interesting to note that in some cases wine—"the blood of the grape"—and the juices of fruits and vegetables, *i.e.* the vehicle of the plant-soul, were used as substitutes for blood.[3] In a later chapter we shall see that herbs and flowers were fabled to grow from the blood of the dead and so to re-embody his spirit, and it will be remembered how Virgil makes the cornel and myrtle which grew upon the grave of Polydorus at once bleed and speak when torn up by the hand of Aeneas.[4] So Ovid, recounting a similar occurrence in the case of the dryads' oak, sacrilegiously felled by Eresicthon, was probably only giving a poetic version of a familiar belief :—

---

[1] W. R. S. Ralston, *Contemporary Review*, vol. xxxi. p. 521.
[2] *Ibid.* vol. xxxi. p. 525.
[3] Robertson Smith, *op. cit.* pp. 126, 213, 461.
[4] *Aeneid*, iii. 27-34.

> He it was
> Whose impious axe mid Ceres' sacred grove
> Dared violate her immemorial shades.
> Huge with the growth of ages in its midst
> An ancient oak there stood, itself a grove,
> With votive tablets hung and grateful gifts
> For vows accomplished. Underneath its shade
> The dryads wove their festal dance.

Eresicthon, in spite of warnings, refused to stay his hand.

> The trembling tree sent forth an audible groan!
> From its pale leaves and acorns died the green,
> Dark oozing sweat from every branch distilled,
> And as the scoffer smote it, crimson-red
> Gushed from the wounded bark the sap, as streams
> When at the altar falls some mighty bull
> The life-blood from his neck.
>
> Then from its heart
> Issued a voice, "Thou strikest in this trunk
> A nymph whom Ceres loves, and for the deed
> Dearly shalt pay. With my last voice thy doom
> I prophesy, and in thy imminent fate
> Find solace for my own."[1]

Mannhardt quotes several mediaeval and modern instances of the belief in bleeding trees.[2] And stories of punishment incurred for destroying a spirit-inhabited tree are not uncommon in folk-lore. There is a German legend of an old crone who attempted to uproot the trunk of an ancient fir-tree. In the midst of her labours a sudden weakness fell upon her, insomuch that she was scarcely able to walk. While endeavouring to crawl home she met a mysterious stranger, who, hearing her story, at once pronounced that in her attempts to uproot the tree she had wounded an elf inhabiting it. If the elf

---

[1] *Metamorphoses*, viii. 741, 774, translated by Henry King (London, 1871).
[2] Mannhardt I. pp. 34 *et seq*.

recovered, he said, so would she; if not, she would die. As the old woman perished that self-same night we are left to infer that the elf died also. From India comes a similar recital. While felling a tree the youthful Satyavant broke out into a profuse sweat, and overcome with sudden weakness, fainted and died upon the spot: he had mortally wounded the indwelling spirit.

Such stories have no doubt arisen from the dread inspired by wood-spirits amongst all people who believe in them. In short, the wild inhabitants of the woods have always retained some of the awe with which their forerunners, the demons, were regarded. Often they are credited with quite a wanton vindictiveness. A Bengal folk-tale tells of a certain banian-tree haunted by spirits who had a habit of wringing the necks of all who ventured to approach the tree by night.[1] In another Indian story a tree that grew beside a Brahman's house was inhabited by a *sankchinni*, a female spirit of white complexion, who one day seized the Brahman's wife and thrust her into a hole in the tree.[2] Sometimes the tree-spirit will be wicked and foolish enough to enter into a human being, and then the exorcist's services are called in. The presence of the spirit is easily discovered. The exorcist has only to set fire to a piece of turmeric root, it being of common knowledge that no spirit can endure the smell of burning turmeric.

The Shánárs of India believe that disembodied spirits haunt the earth, dwelling in trees and taking especial delight in dark forests and solitary places.[3] When a Burman starts upon a journey he hangs a

---

[1] Folkard, *op. cit.* p. 79.   [2] *Ibid.* p. 79.   [3] *Ibid.* p. 79.

branch of plantains or a spray of the sacred *Eugenia* on the pole of his buffalo cart, to conciliate any spirit upon whom he may be unfortunate enough to intrude. The hunter following his lonely quest in the forest will deposit some rice and a little bundle of leaves at the foot of any more than usually majestic tree, hoping thereby to propitiate the *nat* or spirit dwelling therein.[1]

Something of the same fear is felt by the peasants for the fairies, elves, pixies, and all the tribe of little people familiar to European folk-lore. These, too, are all more or less associated with trees, being supposed to dwell either amongst the branches or in the hollow trunks. German elves have a partiality for the oak and elder, and the holes in the trunks are the doorways by which they pass in and out. A similar idea exists amongst the Hindus. Though, as a rule, these forest-elves bear a good character, they are not to be lightly offended, or more will be heard of it. Hence prudent country-folk will never injure trees inhabited by fairies, for when aggrieved they have ample means of avenging themselves by inflicting some malady or causing some ill-luck.

Even in England, especially in Devon and Cornwall, there still exist people who believe that oaks are inhabited by elves—

> Fairy elves, whose midnight revels
> By a forest side or fountain
> Some belated peasant sees.

And it is not yet quite an obsolete custom to turn the coat for luck when passing through elf-haunted groves. It was on St. John's eve that the fairies held their

[1] Folkard, *op. cit.* p. 79.

special revels, and in old days many a timorous hand might be found attaching to his doorway branches of St. John's wort, gathered at midnight on St. John's eve, to protect his dwelling from an invasion of elves. Similarly the peasants living near Mount Etna never sleep beneath trees on St. John's eve, lest the spirits who then issue freely from their leafy dwelling-places should enter into the sleeper.[1]

But it is in Central and North Europe, in the Tyrol and the Vosges, in the German forests, in Russia, Scandinavia, and Finland, that the belief in wood-spirits is most deeply rooted and persistent. Mannhardt, who has diligently collected an enormous mass of evidence on the subject, states that traditions concerning the wild people of the woods are current in all the more wooded countries of Europe. He sees in these traditions an amalgamation of the idea of tree-spirits with that of wind-spirits, and rejects the hypothesis that they arose out of remembrances of savage half-bestial aborigines who took to the woods on the advance of more civilised races.[2] He thus summarises the character of the wild people of Germany, Russia, and Scandinavia. They are often of gigantic proportions, dwell in woods or mountains, and originally were no doubt closely connected with the spirits of trees, their knowledge of "simples" and remedies for sick cattle connecting them with the spirits of vegetation. From head to foot they are clothed in moss, or covered with rough shaggy hair, their long locks floating behind them in the wind. Occasionally they assume an animal form. They announce their presence in the wind and tempest. The male spirits carry as weapons up-

[1] Folkard, *op. cit.* p. 83. [2] Mannhardt I. p. 146.

rooted pines or other trees, and in their fights with each other use tree trunks and pieces of rock. They are almost invariably of a wanton disposition.[1]

Of all the various spirits of the woods, the moss-woman of Central Germany appears to be the most definite example of a tree-spirit. As with the Greek dryad, her life is bound up with that of a tree.[2] The moss-women bear different names and somewhat different characters in different localities, but the following description by the author of *The Fairy Family* represents the common tradition :—

> "A moss-woman," the haymakers cry
> And over the fields in terror they fly,
> She is loosely clad from neck to foot
> In a mantle of moss from the maple's root,
> And like lichen gray on its stem that grows
> Is the hair that over her mantle flows.
> Her skin like the maple-rind is hard,
> Brown and ridgy and furrowed and scarred;
> And each feature flat like the bark we see,
> When a bough has been lopped from the bole of a tree,
> When the newer bark has crept healingly round
> And laps o'er the edge of the open wound;
> Her knotty, root-like feet are bare,
> And her height is an ell from heel to hair.

Sometimes, however, the moss-women and their relatives the wood-maidens are more friendly to man, and will help him industriously in the harvest-field; they have even been known to enter his service and bring prosperity to all his undertakings.

The wild women of Tyrol, known locally as Wild-fanggen, are much more terrifying individuals. Gigantic in stature, their whole body is covered with hair and bristles, and their face distorted with a mouth that stretches from ear to ear. They live together in

---

[1] Mannhardt II. p. 39.   [2] *Ibid.* I. p. 75.

the woods, with which their lives are bound up. If their special wood is destroyed they disappear; if the tree from which a fangga takes her name dies or is felled, she passes out of existence.[1]

The peasants in the Swiss Canton of the Grisons, which by the way has a "wild-man" for its heraldic device, believe in wood-spirits of great strength and agility, who are skilled in weather-lore and the recovery of strayed cattle.[2] The female spirits, some of whom have been known to marry mortals, are clothed in skins; but the males, who are hairy, content themselves with a crown of oak leaves. They are sometimes helpful to men, but more often mischievous, having a propensity for stealing the milk and carrying off the children of the peasants.

The white and green ladies of Franche Comté and Neufchatel belong to the same family, their special proclivity being to entice men away, to drag them through brake and brier, and leave them stripped of their possessions.[3] In Neufchatel there is a rock, "La roche de la Dame Verte," which young men are especially warned to avoid; and in the Jura, a wood where beneath an oak the green ladies are wont to light a fire, and may be heard singing and dancing around it. The peasants when they see the wild flowers and the young corn waving in the wind, whisper to each other that the green lady is passing over them with her companions.

The Swedish conception of the tree-spirit is very similar. He also delights to lead astray those who intrude upon his forest domain. The well-known tendency of man, after losing himself, to wander

[1] Mannhardt I. p. 89.   [2] *Ibid.* I. p. 93.
[3] *Ibid.* I. p. 117.

round and round until he regains his starting-place, is
attributed to the wood-spirit. He looks like a man
when you meet him, but touch him and he shoots to
the height of the loftiest tree. You cry out in terror,
and he laughs " Ha, ha ! " Hunters seek the friendship of these lords of the forest, for he who stands
well with them never misses his aim.[1]

The wood-demon of the Russians, Ljeschi, calls
to mind both classical and modern traditions. He is
of human form, with the horns, ears, and feet of a goat,
his fingers are long claws, and he is covered with
rough hair, often of a green colour. He can assume
many forms, and vary his stature at will ; in the fields
he is no higher than the grass, in the woods as tall
as the trees. Sometimes he is like a man, clothed
in sheepskins, and often, like the cyclops, with only
one eye. Like other wood-demons, he announces his
presence in the storm and the wind. He springs from
tree to tree, and rocks himself in the branches,
screeching and laughing, neighing, lowing, and barking.
He delights to mislead the traveller and plunge him in
difficulties. However unfriendly to man, Ljeschi is on
good terms with animals ; all the birds and beasts of
the wood are under his protection, and the migrations
of squirrels, field-mice, and such small deer are carried
out under his guidance. The peasants are at pains
to propitiate him. In the province of Olonitz the
shepherds offer him a cow every summer, to secure his
favour for the herd ; elsewhere the hunter gives him
the first thing he shoots, leaving it for him in an oak-
wood, or places a piece of bread or pancake strewed
with salt upon a tree stump. There are certain ways of
conjuring his presence and his aid by means of birch-

[1] Mannhardt I. pp. 126 *et seq.*

twigs, or by uttering a given formula while standing on a tree-stump, from which it would appear that he is thought of as dwelling in these vegetable fragments.[1] The Russians also believe in female wood-spirits of terrifying appearance, but they are of less importance than the male.

In the folk-lore of the Finns the spirits of the woods bear a more benign character. The chief of them, "Tapio," is termed "the gracious god of the woodlands," and is represented as very tall and slender, with a long brown beard, a coat of tree moss, and a high-crowned hat of fir leaves. His consort is Mielikki, "the honey rich mother of the woodland," "the hostess of glen and forest." The neighbouring Esthonians have their "grass-mother" who, besides presiding over the home-field, is also queen of the woods.

It is not perhaps singular to find that the traditions with regard to wood-spirits current amongst contiguous peoples should exhibit such a strong resemblance to each other, but when almost exactly the same conceptions are met with in such distant parts as Japan and South America, we can only conclude that the human mind, wherever it exists, is similarly constituted, and, granted the same phenomena, falls back upon the same ideas to explain them.

The Tengus of Japanese legend have many of the characteristic marks of the wood-spirit. They dwell in the topmost branches of lofty trees, are skilled in the language and lore of animals and plants, and are a terror to untruthful children. They have the body of a man, the head of a hawk, with a long proboscis, and powerful claws on their hands; on their feet, also

[1] Mannhardt I. pp. 138 *et seq.*

provided with claws, are stilt-like clogs a foot high. They are hatched from eggs, and in their youth have feathers and wings.[1]

A traveller in Peru only sixty years ago found the tradition of a living wood-ghost, who dwelt in the darkest part of the forest, the haunt of night-birds, and issued forth to decoy the Indians to their destruction.[2] The idea of a wild man of the woods also exists in Brazil. The Indians call him Curupira, and attribute to his agency all such forest sounds as they cannot understand.[3]

Some of the foregoing traditions present a glimpse of the transition towards a later and more highly developed conception, in which the many spirits once believed in become generalised into a single "spirit of vegetation." It is not indeed contended that this belief is necessarily destructive of the earlier. Indeed it is possible that in the loosely working mind of the peasant the two conceptions may exist side by side. The many interesting ceremonies and observances which arose out of this generalised conception will be dealt with in a later chapter.

---

[1] F. Rinder, *Old-World Japan* (London, 1895), p. 137.
[2] Mannhardt I. p. 143.
[3] H. W. Bates, *The Naturalist on the Amazon* (London, 1863), vol. i. p. 73.

CHAPTER IV

THE TREE IN ITS RELATION TO HUMAN LIFE

HAVING dealt with the Tree in its connection on the one hand with gods, and on the other with spirits of more equivocal attributes, we have now to consider a series of myths and traditions wherein it was regarded as entering into a still more intimate relationship with man. Sometimes it was represented as the source from which the human race originally sprang, sometimes, conversely, as the object into which the soul might retreat after death, or into which an individual might be transmuted, body and soul, by some miraculous agency. In other cases the life of a particular tree was held to be bound up with that of an individual or a community, and lastly, in a still larger conception, the tree came to be very widely regarded as the embodiment of the spirit of fertility, the especial patron of the field and flock.

To the modern mind, which claims to have deciphered Nature's scattered hieroglyphs, and finds a genealogical document even in the evanescent wrinkles on a baby's foot, the idea of man taking origin from a tree will seem in the highest degree fantastic, but to the primitive intelligence it probably presented no greater difficulty than the extraction of the new baby from the parsley bed does to the modern child. The early inquirer may well have found in it the most natural answer to the eternal riddle, "Whence came our first parents?" the most plausible solution to the strange problem of man's separate existence upon the globe, supplying the necessary link between him and the great mother-earth, which supported and fed him while alive, and received him again into her bosom when dead. Speculation apart, however, the solution would appear to have commended itself to many different inquirers, for the belief that the human race took its first origin from trees is met with in the mythology of the most widely separated races.

Thus we read in the Eddas that when heaven and earth had been made, Odin and his brothers walking by the sea-shore came upon two trees. These they changed into human beings, male and female. The first brother gave them soul and life; the second endowed them with wit and will to move; the third added face, speech, sight, and hearing. They clothed them also and chose their names, Ask for the man's and Embla for the woman's. And then they sent them forth to be the parents of the human race.[1]

Again, according to the Iranian account of the creation the first human couple, Maschia and Maschiâna, issued from the ground in the form of a rhubarb plant (the *Rheum ribes*), which was at first single, but in process of time became divided into two.[2] Ormuzd imparted to each a human soul, and they became the parents of mankind.

In the corresponding legend current amongst the

[1] *The Prose or Younger Edda*, translated by G. W. Dasent (Stock- holm, 1842), p. 10.
[2] Mannhardt I. p. 7.

Sioux of the Upper Missouri[1] one seems to catch an echo from the Garden of Eden. Here the original parents, like the trees from which they developed, at first stood firmly fixed to the earth, until a monster snake gnawed away the roots and gave them independent motion, just as in Paradise the serpent destroyed the harmony and mutual trust which united Adam and Eve.

The classical nations possessed a similar tradition. According to Hesychius it was believed by the Greeks that the human race was the fruit of the ash, and Hesiod relates that it was from the trunks of ash-trees that Zeus created the third or bronze race of men.[2] The oak was particularised as the favoured tree in another tradition. "Whence art thou?" inquires Penelope of the disguised Ulysses, "for thou are not sprung of oak or rock, as old tales tell."[3] Virgil, too, speaks of

> Nymphs, and fauns, and savage men, who took
> Their birth from trunks of trees and stubborn oak.[4]

The Damaras of South Africa believe that the universal progenitor was a tree, out of which came Damaras, Bushmen, oxen and zebras, and everything else that lives.[5]

In other legends human beings are represented as arising from the tree as its fruit. The first book of the *Mahâbhârata* tells of an enormous Indian fig-tree from whose branches hung little devotees in human form; and an Italian traveller of the fourteenth century was assured by the natives of Malabar that

---

[1] Catlin, *Letters, etc., on North American Indians*, vol. ii. p. 169.
[2] *Works and Days*, v. 143.
[3] *Odyssey*, xix. 162.
[4] *Aeneid*, viii. 315.
[5] F. Galton, *Narrative of an Explorer*, etc. (London, 1853), p. 188.

they knew of trees, which instead of fruit bore pigmy men and women. So long as the wind blew they remained fresh and healthy, but when it dropped they became withered and dry.[1] A somewhat similar tradition was familiar to the Arab geographers, who tell of a talking tree growing at the easternmost point of the habitable world, which bore young women on its branches in place of fruit.[2] And even to the present day folk-tales of Saxony and Thuringia speak of children as "growing on the tree."

In another class of origin-myths *individual* births are represented as taking place directly from a tree. Adonis came forth at the stroke of a sword from the tree into which his mother, the guilty Myrrha, had been transformed in answer to her prayers.[3] The Phrygian Attis, according to one version, was fathered by an almond-tree; while, according to another, his body was confined by Cybele in a pine-tree, from which on the return of spring he was born again.[4] The Khatties of Central India claim to be descended from a certain Khat, "begotten of wood," who, at the prayer of Karna, an illegitimate brother of the five sons of Pându (heroes of the *Mahâbhârata*), sprang from the staff he had fashioned from the branch of a tree to assist him against his legitimate kinsmen.[5]

The above examples prove how widely the conception prevailed that human beings or man-like spirits might owe their first origin to the tree. In a later stage these crude myths were rationalised in three directions. In one the tree came to be, not the

---

[1] Folkard, *op. cit.* p. 117.
[2] Alex. v. Humboldt, *Examen Critique*, vol. i. p. 52.
[3] Apollod. iii. 14, 3.
[4] Goblet d'Alviella, *op. cit.* p. 142.
[5] Folkard, *op. cit.* p. 116.

source, but the scene of a miraculous birth; in another its supposed connection with a human being was explained by a metamorphosis legend; and, thirdly, the tree came to be regarded as the symbol and minister of fecundity.

Many of the gods of Greece were born or brought up, according to tradition, at the foot of some tree, whence Bötticher argues that their worship was founded on a pre-existing tree-cult. Rhea gave birth to Zeus beneath a poplar in Crete, and the ruins of her temple in an adjoining cypress grove were shown even up to the Augustan age.[1] The people of Tanagra asserted that the young Hermes was reared amongst them under a purslane-tree (*andrachnos*), the remains of which were for long treasured in the temple of the god as a sacred souvenir of the institution of his worship.[2] Hera was born and brought up under a willow in Samos, described by Pausanias, who saw it still in leaf, as the most ancient of the sacred trees known to the Greeks.[3] Leto gave birth to Apollo and Artemis in the island of Delos while clasping two trees, by some authorities particularised as an olive and a palm, by others, under the idea that Apollo must have been born at the foot of his own tree, as two laurels.[4] Romulus and Remus were found under the *Ficus ruminalis* by the Tiber, and in later days were worshipped in the Comitium beneath a sapling from that tree. The same idea is met with in the mythology of other nations. Vishnu was born beneath the pillared shade of the banian; Buddha was born and died under a sâl-tree.

The converse of these origin myths is represented

---

[1] Diodor. v. 66.
[2] Pausanias, ix. 22, 2.
[3] *Ibid.* vii. 4, 4; viii. 23, 4.
[4] Servius ad Virgil. *Aeneid*, iii. 91.

in the numerous legends of metamorphosis and transmigration. The well-known story of Apollo and Daphne seems to supply an instance of the way in which the metamorphosis story arose to explain a more primitive connection, the meaning of which had been lost. It is an established fact that the laurel was held sacred in Greece as connected with earth-oracles before the worship of Apollo was introduced. A sacred laurel grew by the prophetic cleft at Delphi in the days when the earth-goddess, Gaia, still presided over the oracle, and according to tradition the goddess' daughter, Daphne, a mountain nymph, was priestess under her.[1] The story which explains the transference of the oracular power from Gaia to Apollo tells how Daphne, fleeing before the god, entreats her mother, Earth, to save her; the ground opens to receive her, and in her place a laurel appears. Apollo, balked of his love, cries: "If thou may'st not be my wife, thou shalt for ever be my tree," and henceforward he makes the laurel his sanctuary, and crowns his head and his lyre with its leaves. Thus he steps into her mother's place, and the laws of Zeus—the old earth-oracles under a new name—are proclaimed through him.

The story is one of the many folk-tales concerning the conversion of mortals into trees which Ovid has so gracefully elaborated in his *Metamorphoses*, and which assume a new importance now that we can trace them back into that old world when tree and man, and indeed all living things, were held to be so near akin. How far they owed their origin to the desire to find a new sanction for the traditional tree-worship by investing it with a human interest, it is impossible to say.

[1] Bötticher, *op. cit.* p. 338.

It is sufficient for us that they demonstrate the survival of very ancient modes of thought amongst races who had otherwise reached a high degree of civilisation. They were amongst the miracles of classical antiquity, and like other miracles, if they prove nothing else, they at least afford invaluable evidence as to the state of mental culture amongst those who found them credible.

One of the most interesting of these metamorphosis legends concerns the fate of the three daughters of the Sun and Clymene, who were so heart-broken at the tragic fate of their brother Phaëton that they were changed into poplars by the banks of the stream into which he had been hurled,—the Eridanus or Po. The tears they shed were preserved in the form of amber :—

> As she bent
> To kneel, Phaëthusa, eldest born, her feet
> Felt stiffen, and Lampetië, at her cry
> Starting, took sudden root, and strove in vain
> For motion to her aid. The third, her hair
> In anguish tearing, tore off leaves! And now
> Their legs grow fixed as trunks, their arms as boughs
> Extend, and upward round them creeps a bark
> That gradual folds the form entire, save yet
> The head and mouth, that to their mother shrieks
> For help. What help is hers to give? Now here,
> Now there she rushes, frantic, kissing this
> Or that while yet she can, and strives to rend
> Their bodies from the clasping bark, and tears
> The fresh leaves from their sprouting heads, and sees,
> Aghast, red drops as from some wound distil.
> And "Ah, forbear!" the sufferer shrieks; "forbear,
> O mother dear! our bodies in these trees
> Alone are rent! Farewell!" And o'er the words,
> Scarce-uttered, closed the bark, and all was still.
> But yet they weep; and in the sun their tears
> To amber harden, by the clear stream caught
> And borne, the gaud and grace of Latian maids.[1]

[1] *Metamorphoses*, ii. 346-366, translated by Henry King (London, 1871).

The story of Baucis and Philemon—the worthy peasants who so hospitably entertained the gods, Zeus and Hermes, disguised as travellers, that their cottage was changed into a temple and they themselves into its priest and priestess—is more familiar. Their prayer that neither should witness the death of the other was fulfilled by the gods, by means of a device familiar enough to the folk-lore of the time:—

> As one morn upon the hallowed steps,
> Bowed now with years, they stood, and to a knot
> Of wondering hearers told the Temple's tale,
> Surprised each saw the other's figure change
> And sprout with sudden verdure: and, as round
> Their forms the rapid foliage spread, while yet
> They could, one mutual fond "Farewell" they took,
> One kiss, and o'er their faces closed the bark,
> And both in trees were hidden! Still the boughs
> That interlacing link the neighbour trunks
> Tyana's peasant loves to show:—the tale
> Her gravest elders—men not like to lie,
> As wherefore should they lie?—with serious faith
> Attested to these ears. The honoured boughs
> Myself have seen with garlands decked, myself
> One garland added more.[1]

In many cases metamorphosis legends were attached to particular kinds of trees, thereby no doubt reinforcing the reverence and affection with which they were regarded. The Greek name for the almond tree, "Phylla," recalled the fate of Phyllis, the beautiful Thracian, who hanged herself in despair when she thought Demophoon had deserted her, and was changed by the gods into one of these trees. Shortly afterwards the truant lover returned, heard the sorrowful tidings, visited the tree, and embraced it with tears. Then suddenly its branches, which till then

---

[1] *Metamorphoses*, viii. 711-724. The story is told by Lelex of Troezene at a feast given to Theseus by Achelous, the river-god.

had remained bare, burst forth into blossom and verdure, as if to show how joyfully conscious they were of the beloved's return. Melus, priest of Aphrodite, filled with grief at the death of his foster-son Adonis, hanged himself, and was changed by the goddess he served into an apple-tree, from which time forward the apple came to be regarded as the most acceptable gift that a lover could offer at her shrine. Lotis, a beautiful nymph, pursued by Priapus, threw herself on the mercy of the gods, and by them was changed into the lotus-tree.

The pine-tree, into which Cybele, in a moment of anger, had changed her lover and devotee, Attis, owed its perennial verdure to the compassion of Zeus for her remorse. The pomegranate was connected in tradition with a certain maid whom Dionysus loved, and the crown-like form of its blossom was accounted for by the story that the god, before he changed her into a tree, had promised her that she should one day wear a crown. The frankincense-tree owed its virtue to the nectar and ambrosia scattered by Apollo on the tomb of Leucothea, who had secured his love, and in consequence had been buried alive at the instance of her rival, Clytia. The tree grew from her grave, and Clytia, pining away in turn from grief, was changed into a plant whose blossoms were destined henceforth, like our sunflower, perpetually to confront the sun, her faithless lover.

The vicarious immortality which the jealous but faithful Clytia thus secured was shared by other fabled personages, many of whom, according to that poetical sentiment which is begotten of all that is gentle and beautiful in nature, were changed into flowers. The idea is indeed a graceful one. For a beautiful youth or maiden, dying young and unhappy, no better recompense than such a flower-change could be imagined by a people, full indeed of the instinctive craving for immortality, but vague in their assurance of a life beyond the grave.

The nymphs who, hearing of the sad death of the beautiful Narcissus, hurried to perform his obsequies, found that he had been changed into a flower, the cup of which was filled with the tears that he had shed. "Bid daffodillies fill their cups with tears," sings Milton, using the old English name for the narcissus. Rhodanthe, the universal praise of whose beauty had aroused the jealous anger of Artemis, was changed by Apollo into the rose. The pipe of Pan was fashioned from the reeds into which the nymph, Syrinx, had been transformed by her sister nymphs in their determination to rescue her from the god's unwelcome overtures.

There are many instances in classical mythology wherein flowers were believed to have arisen from the blood, *i.e.* the very life, of dying persons. The violet sprang from the blood of Attis when Cybele changed him into a pine-tree. From the blood of Hyacinthus, killed in anger by Zephyrus, Apollo caused the hyacinth to grow. Acis, crushed to death by Polyphemus, was changed into a stream, but from his blood there sprang the flowering rush. According to the Egyptians the vine arose from the blood of the Titans.

In other cases tear-drops were, so to speak, the seed of the miracle. The anemone grew from the tears that Aphrodite shed at the death of Adonis :—

G

Woe, woe for Cytherea, he hath perished, the lovely Adonis.
A tear the Paphian sheds for each blood-drop of Adonis,
And tears and blood on the earth are turned to flowers.
The blood brings forth the rose; the tears, the wind-flower;
Woe, woe for Cytherea, he hath perished, the lovely Adonis!"[1]

Shakespeare, it will be remembered, gives to the anemone the magical power of producing love.[2]

The legendary lore of the East contains traditions similar to those above mentioned, of which it will be sufficient to cite the following :—The Burmese believe that the *Canna Indica* or Indian shot sprang from the sacred blood of the Buddha. His evil-minded brother-in-law, incensed at not being allowed to hold a separate assembly of his own, rolled down a rock upon the teacher from a lofty hill. A fragment bruised the Buddha's toe, and drew from it a few drops of blood, from which the sacred plant arose.[3]

In another class of legends, more characteristic of mediaeval than of classical mythology, the *soul* of the dead person was believed to pass into a tree. They are, in fact, cases rather of metempsychosis than of metamorphosis. A legend current in Cornwall tells how, after the loss of her lover, Iseult died broken-hearted, and was buried in the same church with Tristram, but by the king's decree at some distance from him. Soon ivy sprang from either grave, and each branch grew and grew until it met its fellow at the crown of the vaulted roof, and there clasped it and clung to it as only ivy can.[4] In another version the plants that sprang from the graves of the lovers were a rose and a vine. The same idea is met with in the familiar ballad of Fair Margaret and Sweet William.

---

[1] Bion, *Idyl.* i. 63.
[2] *Midsummer Night's Dream*, Act ii. Sc. 2.
[3] Folkard, *op. cit.* p. 268.
[4] *Ibid.* p. 389.

> Margaret was buried in the lower chancel,
>   And William in the higher;
> Out of her breast there sprang a rose,
>   And out of his a brier.
> They grew till they grew into the church top,
>   And then they could grow no higher;
> And there they tyed in a true lover's knot,
>   Which made all the people admire.[1]

A story is told in Japan of a faithful couple who, after enjoying long years of happiness, died at last at the same moment; their spirits withdrew into a tall pine-tree of great age, which a god had once planted as he passed that way. On moonlight nights the lovers may be seen raking together the pine-needles under the tree, which to this day is known as the Pine of the Lovers.[2]

A certain Chinese king had a secretary, Hanpang, for whose young and beautiful wife he conceived a violent passion. Failing in his designs upon her, the king threw Hanpang into prison, where he shortly died of grief. His wife, to escape the royal suit, threw herself from a lofty terrace, having entreated as a last favour that she might be buried beside her husband. The king in his anger ordered otherwise. But that same night a cedar sprang from each grave, and in ten days they had become so tall and vigorous in their growth that they were able to interlace both branch and root, and the people called them the Trees of Faithful Love.[3]

In Germany the following story is told to explain why a certain blue flower, the endive, which grows by the roadside, is called the "Wegewarte" or way-watcher. A maiden, eagerly anticipating the return of her lover from a long voyage, visited every morning

---

[1] Percy's *Reliques*. [2] *Old-World Japan*, p. 115.
[3] Folkard, *op. cit.* p. 274.

and evening the spot where they had parted, and anxiously paced the road, awaiting his coming. At last, worn out by her long vigil, she sank down by the wayside and expired. On the spot where she breathed her last the flower appeared.[1]

There is a Japanese story in which a mother is represented as hearing her dead son's voice in the sighing of a sacred willow which grew above his grave.[2] Grimm quotes other examples.[3] In the song of Roncesvalles, a blackthorn grows above the dead Saracens, a white flower above the dead Christians. In other legends white lilies grow from the graves of persons unjustly executed. From a maiden's grave grew three lilies which none but her lover might pluck.

In all these legends we have a survival of very primitive ideas about the soul, ideas out of which subsequently arose the formal doctrine of transmigration. The immortality of the soul was accepted, but there was always an inclination to quarter it in some new living thing. The instances above given, in which it was thought to pass into some plant, especially concern us, as illustrating the primitive belief that trees and shrubs might contain a spirit in human form.

A further derivative of the assumed kinship between human and vegetable life is the conception of the tree as sympathetically interwoven with the life and fortunes of an individual, a family, or a community. "In folk-tales the life of a person is sometimes so bound up with the life of a plant that the withering of the plant will immediately follow or be followed by the death of the person. Among the M'Bengas in Western Africa, about the Gaboon, when two children are born on the

---

[1] Folkard, *op. cit.* p. 325.   [2] *Old-World Japan*, p. 127.
[3] *Op. cit.* vol. ii. p. 786.

same day the people plant two trees of the same kind and dance round them. The life of each of the children is believed to be bound up with the life of one of the trees, and if the tree dies or is thrown down they are sure that the child will soon die. In the Cameroons, also, the life of a person is believed to be sympathetically bound up with that of the tree. Some of the Papuans unite the life of a new-born child sympathetically with that of a tree, by driving a pebble into the bark of the tree. This is supposed to give them complete mastery over the child's life; if the tree is cut down the child will die."[1] According to the Talmud, the destruction of Bithar, in which four hundred thousand Israelites lost their lives, originated in the resentment of one of its inhabitants at the wanton destruction of a young cedar-tree, which, according to the custom of the place, he had planted at the birth of his child.[2]

It was usual amongst the Romans to plant a tree at the birth of a son, and from its vigour to forecast the prosperity of the child. It is related in the life of Virgil, that the poplar planted at his birth flourished exceedingly, and far outstripped all its contemporaries. A similar superstition has persisted even into times that are almost contemporary. Lord Byron, for all his scepticism, had the idea that his life and prosperity depended on the fate of an oak which he had planted when he first visited Newstead.[3]

The mystical relationship of man and tree is further illustrated in an old German belief quoted by Mannhardt, that a sick child placed in a hole made in a tree by sawing off a branch, or by splitting it open with a

---

[1] Frazer, *op. cit.* vol. ii. p. 328.
[2] *Selections from the Talmud* (London, 1889), p. 318.
[3] Moore's *Life of Lord Byron*, vol. i. p. 101.

wedge, will recover as soon as the tree-wound heals. Should the child die and the tree survive, the human soul will inhabit the tree for the rest of its life.[1]

The family tree and the community tree were merely extensions of this conception. The heroic descendants of Pelops regarded the plane-tree as especially sacred to them and bound up with their fortunes, and in later times we find families taking their names from trees. Mannhardt quotes in this connection the German surnames Linde, Holunder, Kirschbaum, Birnbaum, etc.[2]

But more important than the family tree is the community tree. In many an old German village there stood a tree, often a May-tree, which the villagers guarded as the apple of their eye. It was looked upon as the life-tree, the tutelary genius, the second "I" of the whole community. Devotions were paid to it and gifts offered as to a deity.[3] The ancient fig-tree in the Comitium at Rome, already alluded to as a supposed descendant of the very tree under which Romulus and Remus were found, is another case in point.[4] It was held to be closely connected with the fortunes of the city, and Tacitus describes the terror of the Romans when, in the reign of Nero, it suddenly began to flag and wither, and their relief when, upon the Emperor's death, it was found to have renewed its vigour.[5] Pliny tells of two myrtle-trees, called the Patrician and Plebeian, which grew before the temple of Quirinus at Rome. As sacred to Venus, and hence symbolical of union, these trees were held to represent the amity which existed between the two orders. At

---

[1] Mannhardt I. p. 32.
[2] *Ibid.* p. 53.
[3] *Ibid.* p. 182.
[4] Pliny, *Hist. Nat.* lib. xvi. 27.
[5] Tacitus, *Annal.* xiii. 58.

first they had grown with equal vigour, but when the patricians began to encroach upon the power of the plebs their tree outgrew the other, which languished beneath its baleful shadow. After the Marsian war, however, from which date the power of the Senate began to decline, it was noticed that the patrician tree showed signs of age, while the plebeian sprouted forth with new vigour.[1] Curiously enough, there is, or was so recently as 1885, an old tree in Jerusalem, opposite Cook's office, belonging to an old family and protected by the Sultan's firman, which the Arabs consider will fall when the Sultan's rule ends. "It lost a large limb during the Turco-Russian war, and is now (1885) in a decayed state."[2]

From conceptions such as these the transition is easy to that wider view which regarded the tree as the material representative of the mysterious feminine reproductive power, the good genius of general prosperity. We know that the Semitic nations worshipped under various names a great mother-goddess, the progenitrix of gods and men, and there is evidence to show that the tree was widely venerated as her divine symbol. In the coins of Heliopolis (Baalbek), where this great deity was worshipped under the name of Astarte, the figure of the goddess under the peristyle of her temple is sometimes replaced by a pyramidal cypress. In a coin of Myra, in Lycia, the bust of a goddess is represented in the foliage of a tree. The goddess,

FIG. 24.—Imperial coin of Myra in Lycia, showing tree-goddess.

(Goblet d'Alviella.)

---

[1] Pliny, *op. cit.* lib. xv. 36.
[2] The late General Gordon, in *Times* for 5th January 1885.
[3] Goblet d'Alviella, *op. cit.* p. 142.

who is of the veiled archaic type and wears on her head the *calathus*, the symbol of fertility, is identified by Mr. Farnell with Artemis-Aphrodite, " who is here clearly conceived as a divinity of vegetation."¹ The Canaanites, and under their influence the Israelites, worshipped Ashtaroth, the fruitful goddess, under the symbol of an *ashêra*, a tree or pole, decked with fillets, like the May-tree. An ancient Babylonian cylinder represents a decorated tree with a worshipper beside it, who in the inscription invokes the goddess as her servant.² On other cylinders the tree-symbol sometimes accompanies and sometimes replaces the figure of Istar, the great procreative goddess more or less related to the goddess of the *ashêrim*.³

FIG. 25.—Sacred tree and worshipper.
(Goblet d'Alviella.)

The conception of the tree as the symbol of fertility seems to be still more clearly emphasised in the Assyrian cylinders and bas-reliefs, where it is conventionally represented as a date-palm between two personages, who approach it from either side bearing in their hands a cone similar to the inflorescence of the male date-palm. Mr. Tylor suggests that these personages, variously represented as kings or priests, genii with wings and heads of eagles, or mythical animals, may represent the fertilising winds or divinities, whose procreative influence was typified by the artificial fecundation of the palm, a procedure which is necessary for its successful culture, and which we know from Herodotus to have been familiar to the Babylon-

---

¹ Farnell, *op. cit.* vol. ii. p. 695.   ² J. Menant, *op. cit.* vol. i. p. 220.
³ *Ibid.* vol. i. p. 170 *et seq.*

ians.¹ The design is usually surmounted by the winged disc representing the sun, and the whole is not improbably meant to symbolise the mystery of procreation, in which the male element enshrined in the sun, and the female element inhabiting the tree are appropriately

FIG. 26.—The sacred tree as symbol of fertility.
(From an Assyrian bas-relief. Perrot et Chipiez.)

represented. The same collocation is met with on an altar from the Palmyrene now in Rome, on one of the faces of which is the image of a solar god, and on the other the figure of a cypress with a child carrying a ram amidst its foliage.² In this connection it may be remembered that Apuleius, wishing to paint the

---

¹ Goblet d'Alviella, *op. cit.* p. 145 *et seq.*
² Lajard, *op. cit.* Pl. i.

son of Venus in his mother's lap, is related to have depicted him in the midst of a cypress-tree.

The above facts are important for their bearing on the conception of a tree-inhabiting spirit of vegetation or generalised tree-soul, which, as Mannhardt and Frazer have shown, lies at the root of many otherwise inexplicable observances found amongst the peasantry in different countries and at different periods of history. These customs will be dealt with more fully in a subsequent chapter. In all of them we find a tree, or the branch of a tree, or a human being or puppet dressed to represent a tree, figuring as the symbol or representative of a spirit who is regarded as more or less friendly to man, and endowed with the power of assisting his material prosperity. In more primitive times than the present this prosperity resolved itself into a question of fecundity, and the power which could make the fields to bear, the flocks to multiply, and women to give increase, naturally held the foremost place in the affections of the people. The rich and the cultured found other attributes to worship and other gods to personify them, but the peasant clung to the observances by which the spirit of fertility was propitiated. Hence the tree, long after it had ceased to be worshipped as the home of the great gods, or to be regarded as the parent of mankind, still held a firm place in the devotions of the people as the embodiment of the all-powerful patron of universal fertility.

Of the innumerable observances founded on this idea the following may be taken as a sample. The sacred chili or cedar of Gilgit, on the north-western frontier of India, was held to have the power of causing the herds to multiply and women to bear children. At the commencement of wheat-sowing three chosen unmarried youths, who had undergone purification for three days, started for the mountains where the cedars grew, taking with them wine, oil, and bread, and fruit of every kind. Having found a suitable tree they sprinkled the oil and wine on it, while they ate the bread and fruit as a sacrificial feast. Then they cut off a branch and brought it to the village, where amid general rejoicing it was placed on a large stone beside running water. A goat was then sacrificed and its blood poured over the cedar branch, while the villagers danced around it. The goat's flesh was eaten, and every man went to his house bearing a spray of cedar. On his arrival he said to his wife, "If you want children I have brought them to you; if you want cattle I have brought them; whatever you want, I have it."[1]

The same idea is no doubt to be traced in the form of survival, in the custom of giving a branch of laurel to a bride which is found, according to Mannhardt, at Carnac in Brittany;[2] in the introduction of a decorated pine-bough into the house of the bride, met with in Little Russia, as well as in the ceremony of "carrying the May," adorned with lights, before the bride and bridegroom in Hanoverian weddings.[3]

The day of these observances is past, but underlying them there was a vital and still valid truth. To us as to the ancients the tree is still the patron of fertility, as those have discovered to their cost who have bared a country of its forests. To us as to them it is still the thing of all things living that is endowed with the most enduring life, the most persistent vigour.

---

[1] Frazer, *op. cit.* vol. i. p. 70.   [2] Mannhardt I. p. 222.
[3] *Ibid.* p. 46.

Generations come and go, but the tree lives on and every spring puts forth new leaves, and every autumn bears new seed, and even to its last decrepitude the leaves are as green and the seeds as full of life as in the prime of its youth. What changes has not the oldest tree in England witnessed! In the southern counties there is an ancient way, once thronged by travellers, but now deserted and broken in its continuity; yet to this day, even where parks and pastures have overlain it, its course may still be traced by the yew-trees planted at its side by pilgrims journeying to the shrine of St. Thomas of Canterbury, in the days when their brothers were fighting for the White Rose or the Red.

CHAPTER V

THE TREE AS ORACLE

AMONGST the innumerable sources from which the nations of antiquity professed to derive knowledge of futurity and practical guidance in the affairs of life the tree held a very prominent place. Tree-oracles formed, indeed, the natural corollary of tree-worship, and their number and popularity provide additional testimony to the genuineness and extent of the ancient belief that certain trees were tenanted by a supernatural essence. For it was as "animated demoniac beings," to use Robertson Smith's phrase, that trees possessed oracular virtue. It was the god dwelling in them who produced the mysterious rustlings and movements of the branches, from which the responses were interpreted by the attendant priests. But according to the ancient view the tree derived a further title to its oracular prestige from its connection by means of its roots with the under-world, the mysterious abode of departed spirits, in whom wisdom and knowledge of the future were supposed to be vested. Thus the special prophetic power attributed to the variety of oak (probably the *Quercus esculus*) which grew at Dodona was ascribed by later writers to the fact that its roots pierced the earth more deeply than those of other trees, reaching down even to Tartarus (*tantum radice in Tartara*).¹ It was from this under-world that Saul summoned Samuel, and it was in the hope of obtaining help from the spirit of some dead hero by means of a dream, that men were wont to pass the night at his tomb or his temple. The modern Arabs who still worship certain sacred trees, as the place where angels or *jinni* descend, believe that a sick man who sleeps under such a tree will receive counsel in a dream for the restoration of his health.²

Of organised oracles the earliest was no doubt the earth oracle, and the part played in the ceremonial by natural fissures, springs, and trees probably grew out of their close connection with the earth. The most famous oracle of antiquity, that of Delphi, was situated at the opening of a natural cleft in the rock, believed to be at the very centre of the earth, and was originally presided over by the great earth-mother, Gaia, the subordinate part played by the laurel which once grew near the cleft being expressed by the legend that Daphne was the daughter and priestess of Gaia.³ The procedure at another famous oracle, that of Trophonius at Lebadea, near Mount Helicon in Boeotia, was distinctly modelled on the idea of a descent into the under-world,⁴ the suppliant obtaining his answer in a cave, where his experiences were so terrible that he never smiled again; whence it came to be said of any particularly lugubrious individual that he had consulted the oracle of Trophonius. A still more striking illustration of the antiquity of this conception is found in the account of the initiation of

---

[1] Virgil, *Georg.* ii. 291; Servius ad Virgil. *Aeneid*, iv. 446.
[2] Robertson Smith, *op. cit.* p. 169.
[3] Pausanias, x. 5, 3.
[4] *Encyclop. Brit.*, 9th edition, vol. xvii. p. 808.

an augur given on a Babylonian tablet in the British Museum. The candidate is there made to descend into an artificial imitation of the lower world, where he beholds "the altars amidst the waters, the treasures of Anu, Bel, and Ea, the tablets of the gods, the delivering of the oracle of heaven and earth, and the cedar-tree, the beloved of the great gods."[1] Here the earth-oracle and the tree-oracle are seen in very early conjunction; but the belief in the divine power inherent in the tree can be traced still farther back, for in a bilingual text of much earlier date we read of "the cedar-tree, the tree that shatters the power of the incubus, upon whose core is recorded the name of Ea," *i.e.* the god of wisdom.[2]

The idea of the tree-oracle was familiar to other branches of the Semitic race, and is expressed in their common tradition of a tree of knowledge. Several allusions to oracular trees are met with in the Old Testament. That Jehovah should speak to Moses out of the burning-bush, if not to be regarded as a case in point, was at any rate quite in conformity with surrounding tradition, for there is no doubt that the belief in trees as places of divine revelation was very prevalent in Canaan. The famous holy tree near Shechem, called the tree of the soothsayers in Judges ix. 37, and the tree or trees of the revealer in Genesis xii. 6 and Deuteronomy xi. 30, must have been the seat of a Canaanite tree-oracle.[3] The prophetess Deborah gave her responses under a palm near Bethel, which, according to sacred tradition, marked the grave of the nurse of Rachel. And David, when he inquired of the Lord as to the right moment for

---

[1] Sayce, *op. cit.* p. 241.   [2] *Ibid.* p. 240.
[3] Robertson Smith, *op. cit.* p. 179.

attacking the Philistines, received the signal in "the sound of a going in the tops of the mulberry-trees."[1] The *ashéra* or artificial tree in which the deity was supposed to dwell also appears to have been used by the Canaanites for the purposes of divination, a practice probably alluded to in the rebuke of the prophet, "My people ask counsel at their stock, and their staff declareth unto them."[2]

But by far the most striking instance of a tree-oracle, and perhaps one may even say the most signal vestige of the primitive tree-worship, was the oracle of the Pelasgic Zeus at Dodona in Epirus. Here in a grove of oaks there was a very ancient tree, believed to be the actual seat of the deity, whose responses were interpreted from the rustling of its branches, from the murmur of the sacred spring which welled forth at its foot, or from the drawing of the oracle lots kept in an urn beneath it. The origin of the oracle is lost in prehistoric gloom; probably it existed earlier than the worship of Zeus himself. Homer makes Ulysses visit it,[3] and Hesiod states that Zeus dwelt there in the trunk of a tree.[4] Herodotus affirms, on the testimony both of the priestesses of Dodona and of the Egyptian priests at Thebes, that the oracle was introduced from Egypt, and adds that the manner in which oracles were delivered at Thebes and at Dodona was very similar. The priests at Thebes told him that two women employed in their temple had been captured by Phoenicians, and sold the one into Libya, the other to the Greeks; the former established the oracle of Zeus Ammon in the Libyan desert, the latter that of Dodona. In the account given him by the

[1] 2 Samuel v. 24.
[2] Hosea iv. 12 (R. V.).
[3] *Odyssey*, xiv. 327.
[4] Scholiast on Sophocles, *Trachiniae* 1169.

Dodonaean priestesses, it was asserted that the oracles were founded by two black pigeons from Thebes.[1] We know from other sources that the oracle of Zeus-Ammon was vested in an ancient tree (γεράνδρυον).[2] But whatever may have been its origin there is no doubt that the oracle of Dodona had a long and active career, continuing for close upon two thousand years. Silius Italicus, towards the end of the first century A.D., reiterates the statement of Hesiod that the deity at Dodona occupied a tree;[3] Pausanias a hundred years later found the tree still green and flourishing,[4] and Philostratos about the same time saw it adorned with wreaths and sacred fillets, "because, like the Delphic tripod, it gave forth oracles."[5] A later writer states that the oracular voices ceased on the felling of the tree by a certain Illyrian bandit,[6] but there is evidence that the tree and the oracle were still in existence in the middle of the fourth century A.D. These ancient testimonies to the importance of the oracle have been marvellously corroborated by the discovery in the course of recent excavations of a large number of leaden tablets inscribed with the questions addressed to the god by his votaries, and dating from 400 B.C. onwards.[7]

According to classical mythology, the oracular virtue of the famous oak of Dodona was not only transmitted to its offshoots, but even preserved in the dead wood after its separation from the tree. Ovid, in relating the story of the plague of Aegina, tells how Aeacus, standing beneath

---

[1] Herodotus, ii. 52, 57.
[2] Clem. Alex., *Protrept.* ii. 11.
[3] Silius Ital. vi. 691.
[4] Pausanias, viii. 23, 4; i. 17, 5.
[5] Philostrat. *Imag.* ii. 33.
[6] Servius ad Virgil. *Aen.* iii. 466.
[7] *Encyclop. Brit.*, 9th edition, vol. xvii. p. 809. Cf. also Farnell, *op. cit.* vol. i. p. 40.

> A branching oak, the Sire's own tree, from seed
> Of old Dodona sprung,

calls upon Zeus to repeople his stricken kingdom, and fill his desolate walls anew with citizens as numerous as the ants at his feet.

> Not a breath
> Was stirring, but the branches shook, the leaves
> With rustling murmur waved.

Accepting the omen he kisses the sacred tree, falls asleep beneath it, and wakes to find that the ants have been miraculously changed into men, the famous Myrmidons.[1] Again, it is related by more than one author that when the good ship *Argo* was built, Athena introduced into it by way of amulet a beam hewn in the grove of Dodona, which in the subsequent voyage constantly gave the Argonauts warning and advice.[2]

At the famous oracle of Delphi the tree played as intrinsic, if not so predominant, a part as at Dodona, its function being shared by the fissure in the earth and the sacred spring, which testify to the chthonic origin of the oracle, whilst the use of the sacred tripod has been thought to connect it with the class of fire oracles.[3] There is evidence that a laurel-tree grew beside the oracular fissure in Gaia's time,[4] and, according to tradition, the earliest temple of Apollo was a hut of laurel boughs erected by the god's own hands.[5] And later on, when the original tree had disappeared and the fissure had been enclosed in the Adytum, the entrance to the latter, as well as the tripod on which the Pythia sat, were hidden in fresh laurel leaves

---

[1] *Metam.* vii. 622-654
[2] Apollod. i. 9, 16; Philostrat. *Imag.* ii. 15.
[3] Bötticher, *op. cit.* p. 341.
[4] Euripides, *Hecuba*, 456.
[5] Bötticher, *op. cit.* p. 344.

whenever the oracle was given, and the priestess having chewed laurel leaves and crowned herself with a wreath of the sacred plant, waved a laurel branch while chanting her ecstatic utterances. Every ninth year, moreover, a bower of laurel branches was erected in the forecourt of the temple. It is uncertain how far Apollo's close connection with the laurel may have originated from Delphi, but it is a fact that in later times his oracular function was inseparably bound up with the use of that tree, and the laurel became the recognised instrument of prophecy (*per lauros geomantis*). And at Delphi, when the laurel trees had disappeared, the oracle ceased, for the messenger sent by the Emperor Julian to reinaugurate it received for answer, "Tell the king that the cunningly-built chamber has fallen to the ground; Apollo no longer has bower, or inspired laurel, or prophetic spring; vanished is the talking water."[1]

To pass briefly over other examples of tree-oracle, in Armenia the fire-priests were wont to interpret the will of the god from the movements observed in the branches of the holy plane-tree at Armavira.[2] The Chaldaeo-Assyrians read the future in the rustling of the leaves of the prophetic trees.[3] At Nejrân, in Yemen, the Arabs professed to obtain oracles from the spirit who inhabited a sacred date-palm.[4]

In the Sháh Námeh, Firdausi, working no doubt upon an ancient tradition, tells how Sikander, or Alexander the Great, consulted a tree-oracle in Persia.[5] "From thence he proceeded to another city,

---

[1] Bötticher, *op. cit.* p. 344.
[2] Moses Choren, *Hist. Armen.* i. 15, 19.
[3] F. Lenormant, *La Divination chez les Chaldéens* (Paris, 1875), p. 85.
[4] Sir W. Ouseley, *Travels*, vol. i. p. 369.
[5] The Sháh Námeh, *Chandos Classics*, p. 336.

where he was received with great homage by the most illustrious of the nation. He inquired of them if there were anything wonderful or extraordinary in their country, that he might go to see it, and they replied that there were two trees in the kingdom, one a male, the other a female, from which a voice proceeded. The male tree spoke in the day and the female tree in the night, and whoever had a wish went thither to have his desires accomplished. Sikander immediately repaired to the spot, and approaching it, he hoped in his heart that a considerable part of his life still remained to be enjoyed. When he came under the tree a terrible sound arose and rang in his ears, and he asked the people present what it meant. The attendant priest said it implied that fourteen years of his life still remained. Sikander at this interpretation of the prophetic sound wept, and the burning tears ran down his cheeks. Again he asked, 'Shall I return to Rúm and see my mother and children before I die?' and the answer was, 'Thou wilt die at Kashán.'"

Amongst the Romans other forms of augury appear to have taken the place of the old tree-oracles and reduced them to comparative insignificance. The most important of those that remained was the prophetic ilex grove upon the Aventine hill, sacred to Faunus and Picus. Hither the applicant came, fasting and meanly clothed, and having crowned himself with beech leaves, sacrificed two sheep to the deities of the grove, and laying himself down upon their pelts, awaited the counsel of the gods in his dream.[1] There was another grove oracle of Faunus at Tibur by the Albunean spring,[2] and at the neighbouring Preneste,

[1] Ovid, *Fasti*, iii. 294.   [2] *Ibid.* iv. 650; Virgil, *Aeneid*, vii. 81.

where the oracle of Jupiter was held in great repute, the oracle lots were fashioned from the wood of his sacred oak.[1] At the more sequestered Tiora Matiena the tree-oracle appears to have dwindled into a mere vestige, the responses being given by a woodpecker perched upon an oaken column.[2]

To tree-omens, as distinguished from tree-oracles, the Romans attached much importance, and they possessed several treatises dealing with such portents. The family and community tree described in the last chapter had a certain oracular character, and foretold in its own fortunes the prosperity or adversity of those whom it represented. The withering of the laurel grove of Augustus was held to portend the death of Nero, and with him the extinction of the Augustan house and its adopted members; the fall of Vespasian's cypress foretold the death of Domitian. If the sacred tree attached to a sanctuary were uprooted by the wind, it was a clear proof that the deity had withdrawn his protection, and unless the tree upreared itself anew, his worship at that spot was discontinued. The Sibylline books contained explicit instructions with regard to these eventualities and were invariably consulted in every such case. Innumerable instances of these tree-omens are given in classical literature.[3]

The legends of trees which spoke intelligibly belong rather to myth than to history, but they were quite in accordance with the ancient belief that any tree which contained a tree-soul, were it the spirit of a god or only that of a dryad, might express itself in words. Thus the spirits inhabiting the three trees of the Hesperides gave advice to the wandering

---

[1] Cicero, *De Divinat.* ii. 40. [2] Dion. Halic. i. 14.
[3] Bötticher, *op. cit.* chap. xi.

Argonauts. Philostratus relates that at the command of Apollonius a tree addressed him in a distinct female voice.[1] When Rome was invaded by the Gauls a voice from out of the grove of Vesta warned the Romans to repair their walls or their city would fall.[2] And after the battle in which Brutus and Aruns Tarquinius slew each other, a powerful voice from the neighbouring grove of Arsia announced that the victory lay with the Romans.[3] A later instance is that of the *gharcad* tree which spoke to Moslim b. 'Ocba in a dream, and designated him to the command of the army of Yazīd against Medina.[4]

It has already been mentioned that the responses at Dodona were sometimes interpreted from the oracle lots kept in an urn that stood upon a sacred table beneath the tree, and the same form of divination was also apparently in use at Delphi,[5] whilst at Preneste it was the sole method employed. Indeed this outgrowth of the tree-oracle was in common use throughout the ancient world. There is a probable allusion to it in Ezekiel xxi. 21. The Scythian soothsayers were wont to divine by the help of a number of willow rods, which they placed upon the ground, uttering their predictions as they gathered them up one by one. They also practised divination by means of the bark of the linden-tree.[6] Amongst the neighbouring Alani, in Sarmatia, women foretold the future by means of straight rods cut with secret enchantments at certain times and marked very carefully.[7] The Germans used to divine by means of the fragments of a branch cut from a fruit-tree, which

---

[1] Bötticher, *op. cit.* p. 164.
[2] Cicero, *De Divinat.* i. 45.
[3] Dion. Halic. v. 16.
[4] Robertson Smith, *op. cit.* p. 126.
[5] Bötticher, *op. cit.* p. 113, note 22.
[6] Herodotus, iv. 67.
[7] Ammian. Marcell. L. 31.

they threw on to a white cloth.¹ The omen sticks of the Druids, frequently referred to in the Bardic poems, were probably rods cut from a fruit-tree and marked with mystical emblems.²

It is not easy to define the exact connection between these oracle-lots and that strange survival, the divining-rod, but it may be taken for certain that the belief in the efficacy of the latter is "a superstition cognate to the belief in sacred trees,"³ and that the idea underlying both the oracle-lot and the divining-rod was that they were animated by an indwelling spirit, probably by the spirit of the tree from which they were cut. We know from Pliny and Pausanias that the earliest images of the gods were made of wood, and that the Greeks, Romans, and other pre-Christian nations worshipped stakes or peeled rods of wood, painted, or dressed, or roughly carved in the semblance of an anthropomorphic god, and supposed to be inhabited by a divine essence. It was probably by a similar mode of reasoning that the spear, the sceptre, the staff of the general, the standards of the army, the herald's wand, the rods of the flamens, the lituus of the augur, and the truncheon of the constable came to be symbolically representative of power and inviolability, the primitive assumption being that they retained some of the divine spirit resident in the tree from which they were cut.⁴ From a similar parentage sprang the popular custom of striking men, cattle, and plants with a green switch (Lebensrute) at certain seasons of the year in order to make them fruitful, an

---

¹ Tacitus, *Germ.* x.
² E. Davies, *Celtic Researches*, p. 812; *British Druids*, p. 43.
³ R. Smith, *op. cit.* p. 179, note 5.
⁴ The whole subject is very fully treated by Bötticher, *op. cit.* chap. xvi.

observance of which so many instances have been collected by Mannhardt. "It was the tree-soul, the spirit of vegetation," he concludes, "communicated by means of this switching, which drove away the demons of sickness and sterility and evoked fruitfulness and health."[1] The divining-rod is, if one may say so, first cousin to the "life-rood." Each represents and embodies a different function of the supernatural—the one its procreative, the other its prophetic attribute. The divining-rod is the meagre survival of the once renowned tree-oracle.

It may seem strange that in this positive age there should exist people calling themselves educated, who believe that a stick cut from a hazel or thorn-bush may in the hands of a specially endowed person possess a magical power of revealing the secrets of the earth. But so it is. There are in this country at the present hour some half-dozen professional experts, who claim the faculty of discovering unsuspected springs of water by means of the divining-rod, and furnish well-attested instances of their success. It is not necessary to discuss the credibility of their assertions or to formulate a theory to account for their success. The subject of the divining-rod concerns us only in so far as it is a vestige—a poor and atrophied vestige—of the magic eloquence once associated with the sacred tree. It is impossible to say when the use of the divining-rod first originated. It is mentioned in the Vedas, and is well known to have flourished amongst the Chaldaeans and Egyptians. But in those early days the function of the magical rod was not restricted, as it was later and is now, to the search for water or buried treasure. The Greeks and Romans

[1] Mannhardt I. p. 303.

found many uses for it. Cicero speaks of providing for one's wants, *quasi virgulâ divinâ, ut aiunt.* It was a familiar instrument in the hands of the British Druids, and is still largely employed in China. Mediaeval writers speak of it as being in very common use among the miners of Germany.[1]

At all times and in all places the act of cutting and preparing the rod has been the subject of much ceremony. It had to be severed at a particular moment, and from a particular kind of tree, the latter varying according to the country. As a rule a fruit-tree, or some other tree that was useful and beneficent to man, was chosen. The Chinese prefer the peach; the Druids made choice of the apple-tree.[2] Elsewhere the hazel, the willow, and the black-thorn have been selected, and the last-named is still known in Germany as the "wishing-thorn," as it is the tree from which wishing-rods were cut. The time at which the rod was cut was equally important. For centuries the Chinese have adhered to the first new moon after the winter solstice as the most favourable date for the ceremony. The French custom was to cut it on Mercury's day (Wednesday) at the planetary hour of Mercury.[3] In Sweden divining-rods of mistletoe are cut on midsummer eve.[4] Even in comparatively modern times believers in the divining-rod professed to expect more of a rod which had been cut between sunset and sunrise, upon some holy day or at new moon, from a branch on which the rising sun first shone.[5]

These mystic observances smack of a far-distant past, and the modern water-finder appears to have

---

[1] De Vallemont, *Physique occulte* (1696), p. 10.
[2] Folkard, *op. cit.* p. 113.
[3] John O'Neill, *The Night of the Gods*, vol. i. p. 53.
[4] Frazer, *op. cit.* vol. ii. p. 367.
[5] Folkard, *op. cit.* p. 114.

discarded them. His practice is to cut a forked branch about eighteen inches in length from any convenient hazel or white-thorn bush, and grasping the prongs very firmly between the thumb and two first fingers of each hand, the joint being held downwards, he walks over the ground where it is desired to find water. If he approaches a hidden spring, the joint will begin to rise against his will, and when he has reached it, will make a complete half revolution, breaking or bending the twigs held in his hands, until the joint is uppermost. The depth of the spring is estimated by the force with which the rod is repelled from it. The mental exhaustion of the operator after a successful operation is said to be considerable. In an old volume of the *Quarterly Review* (No. 44) an account is given of a certain Lady Noel who was skilful in the use of the divining-rod. She used a thin forked hazel-twig, which immediately bent when she came over the underground spring, its motion being more or less rapid as she approached or withdrew from the spot. "When just over it the twig turned so quick as to snap, breaking near the fingers, which by pressing it were indented and heated and almost blistered. A degree of agitation was also visible in her face."

Many of the superstitious practices that still survive in remote villages are no doubt of the same ancestry as the divining-rod. In the valley of Lanzo in Piedmont, lovers in doubt whether to marry consult the oracle in the form of a herb called *concordia*, the root of which is shaped like two hands, each with its five fingers. If the herb they find has the hands conjoined, the omen is favourable; but unfavourable if the hands point different ways.[1]

[1] A. de Gubernatis, *op. cit.* vol. i. p. 99.

The following naïve recital is quoted in Brand's antiquities :—" Last Friday was Valentine's day, and the night before I got five bay-leaves, and pinned four of them to the four corners of my pillow, and the fifth to the middle ; and then, if I dreamt of my sweetheart, Betty said we should be married before the year was out."[1] This belief in the magical power of certain leaves is enshrined in many jingles, still found in the rustic formulary, such as—

> The even ash-leaf in my glove
> The first I meet shall be my love ;[2]

or

> Find even ash or four-leaved clover
> And you'll see your true love before the day's over.[3]

In old days on St. Valentine's eve many a rustic maid has sprinkled bay-leaves with rose-water and laid them across her pillow, and then lying down in a clean night-gown, turned wrong side out, has softly recited—

> Good Valentine, be kind to me,
> In dreams let me my true love see ;[4]

or, if she were a Staffordshire lass, she probably preferred St. Thomas's eve, and having placed a sprig of evergreen under her pillow, sighed—

> Good St. Thomas, stand by my bed
> And tell me when I shall be wed.[5]

To those who are new to the subject of comparative mythology these doggrels whispered by foolish country

---

[1] J. Brand, *Observations on the Popular Antiquities of Great Britain* (London, 1849), vol. i. p. 58.
[2] W. Hone, *Year Book* (1878), p. 588.
[3] W. Henderson, *Folk-lore of the Northern Counties*, pp. 110, 111.
[4] J. O. Halliwell, *Popular Rhymes and Nursery Tales* (1849), pp. 219, 220.
[5] C. H. Poole, *Customs, Legends, and Superstitions of Staffordshire*, p. 74.

girls under the stress of a natural impulse may seem absurdly irrelevant. But to that science which strives to unravel the beliefs and ideas of long dead people, every vestige, every survival is important. The charms above mentioned did not spring, fully matured, from the brain of some peculiarly inventive dairy-maid. They have a long, long pedigree, and, like the zebra stripe which will sometimes appear on a pure-bred horse, they throw us back to an age when man believed that the world was controlled by spirits, and that he, like everything else, was but a puppet in their hands.

CHAPTER VI

THE UNIVERSE-TREE

ONE of the most interesting points in connection with tree myths is the wide distribution of the conception of the cosmogonic or world-tree, of which the Scandinavian Yggdrasil is the most familiar example. The idea is met with amongst the ancient Chaldaeans, the Egyptians, the Persians, the Hindus, and the Aryan races of Northern Europe, as well as in the mythology of China and Japan; and this community of tradition has been regarded by some authorities as pointing to a prehistoric intercourse between these widely-separated races, if not to their common origin.[1] But, apart from the fact that the same conception is also found in a rudimentary form amongst the aborigines of New Zealand and America, it is not difficult to imagine that it may have occurred separately to more than one inquirer. In short, "the idea of referring to the form of a tree the apparent conformation of the universe is one of the most natural methods of reasoning which can occur to the savage mind."[2] The moment he began to concern himself with such questions, the primitive thinker must have asked himself why the heavenly firmament, with its sun and stars

[1] Goblet d'Alviella, *op. cit.* p. 169.   [2] *Ibid.* p. 171.

and the waters above it, did not fall to earth like everything else within his knowledge. His mind naturally demanded some prop or support to antagonise what in his experience was the unrestricted despotism of geocentric gravitation. The Egyptian explained the problem by representing the sky as the star-spangled body of the goddess Nûit, who had been separated from her husband Sibû, the earth, by the efforts of Shû. In the mythology of the Maoris, Rangi, the sky, was forcibly separated from his wife, the universal mother, earth, by one of their children, Tane Mahuta, father of forests, who planting his head upon the earth, upheld the heavens with his feet.[1]

The fact that the celestial bodies were observed to revolve around a fixed point rendered it a necessity that this assumed support of the heaven should be of the nature of a central axis, upholding the sky-roof as the pole upholds a tent. To the inhabitants of mountainous countries, who saw the clouds resting upon the peaks, the idea of a heaven-supporting mountain no doubt presented itself as the most reasonable solution. Thus Aristotle, to quote Lord Bacon, " elegantly expoundeth the ancient fable of Atlas (that stood fixed and bare up the heaven from falling) to be meant of the poles or axle-tree of heaven." To plain-dwellers, however, the tree was the loftiest object within their experience, and it may be conjectured that the idea of a central world-supporting tree was a product of the lowlands. In some cases the two conceptions were combined and the world-tree was placed on the summit of a world-mountain. It is interesting, however, to note that the earliest known version of a world-tree, pure and simple, comes to us from the fertile

[1] Sir G. Grey, *Polynesian Mythology* (London, 1855), p. 1.

alluvial plain on the borders of the Persian Gulf. The
account, contained in an old bilingual hymn, and probably of Accadian origin, represents the tree as growing
in the garden of Edin or Eden, placed by Babylonian
tradition in the immediate vicinity of Eridu, a city
which flourished at the mouth of the Euphrates
between 3000 and 4000 B.C.

In Eridu a stalk grew overshadowing; in a holy place did it become
 green;
Its roots were of white crystal, which stretched towards the deep.
(Before) Ea was its course in Eridu, teeming with fertility;
Its seat was the (central place of the earth);
Its foliage (?) was the couch of Zikum the (primaeval) mother.
Into the heart of its holy house, which spread its shade like a forest,
 hath no man entered.
(There is the home) of the mighty mother who passes across the sky.
In the midst of it was Tammuz.
There is the shrine of the two (gods).[1]

Of this glorified tree or stem it is to be observed
that it grew at the centre of the earth; that its roots
pierced down into the abysmal watery deep, where the
amphibious Ea, the god of wisdom, had his seat, and
whence he nourished the earth with springs and
streams; that its foliage supported Zikum, the primordial heavens, and overshadowed the earth, which
was apparently regarded as a plane placed midway
between the firmament above and the deep below.
The stem itself was the home of Davkina, consort of
Ea, the great mother, "the lady of the Earth," and of
her son Tammuz, a temple too sacred for mortals to
enter.

Even were it not to be inferred from other evidence,
there could be little doubt that the people amongst
whom the above conception arose must have been

---

[1] A. H. Sayce, *op. cit.* p. 238.

already familiar with tree-worship. The mighty stem, in which the great gods dwelt, was but a poetical amplification of the sacred, spirit-inhabited tree, and arose out of the same idealising process as that which gave birth to the nearly related tree of knowledge and tree of life.

Side by side with that of a world-tree the conception of a world-mountain is also met with in the primitive cosmogony of the Chaldaeans, but while the former tradition belonged to Sumir or Southern Babylonia, the latter seems to have prevailed in the Northern Accad, whose inhabitants had once been mountain-dwellers.[1] This "mountain of the world," "whose head rivalled the heaven," which had the pure deep for its foundation and was the home of the gods, was placed in the north, and its worship survived in that of the "illustrious mounds" of the Babylonian plain, which were equally regarded as the visible habitation of divine spirits. Isaiah represents the king of Babylon as boasting, "I will ascend into heaven, I will exalt my throne above the stars of God; and I will sit upon the mount of congregation, in the uttermost parts of the north."[2] It seems clear that the prophet is alluding to the myth of a Chaldaean Olympus, where the gods held their assemblies. In one of the Babylonian hymns this mountain is addressed as, "O thou who givest shade, Lord who castest thy shadow over the land, great mount,"[3] from which it might appear that the idea of the world-mountain was not very strictly dissociated from that of a world-tree.

In the corresponding cosmogony, which was current five thousand years later amongst the Scandinavians,

---

[1] A. H. Sayce, *op. cit.* p. 362.   [2] Isaiah xiv. 13.
[3] De Gubernatis, *op. cit.* vol. i. p. 45.

the two conceptions were unequivocally combined. The Norse Yggdrasil, in spite of the many quaint symbolical fancies which have been embroidered on to the main conception, represents such a remarkable amalgamation of ideas originally Oriental that it is difficult to believe that it can have had a totally independent origin. The world-mountain, the world-tree with the birds in its branches, and the connection of the latter with another peculiarly Eastern idea, that of the food of the gods, are all reproduced in the cosmogonic traditions of the Eddas, and it is highly probable that they formed part of a primitive folk-lore common to the different races. As their culture grew the Chaldaeans gave up their earlier conception, and came to regard the earth as a gigantic bowl floating bottom upwards upon the deep, but to the Norse poet the world still remained a flat disc surrounded by a river ocean, and limited by mountain ranges. In its centre Asgard, the mountain of the gods, was pierced by a mighty tree trunk, the branches of which overshadowed the world and supported the sky, the stars, and the clouds, whilst its roots stretched downwards into the primordial abyss. The apples stored in Valhal, by eating which the gods preserved their youth, closely correspond to the amrita or soma which, as we shall see, was a peculiar feature of the Eastern conception of the world-tree.

"The chief and most holy seat of the gods," say the Eddas, "is by the ash Yggdrasil. There the gods meet in council every day. It is the greatest and best of all trees, its branches spread over all the world and reach above heaven. Three roots sustain the tree and stand wide apart: one is with the Asa; the second with the Frost-giants; the third reaches into Niflheim, and under it is Hvergelmer, where Nidhug gnaws the root from below. But under the second root, which extends to the Frost-giants, is the well of Mimer, wherein knowledge and wisdom are concealed. The third root of the ash is in heaven, and beneath it is the most sacred fountain of Urd. Here the gods have their doomstead. The Asa ride thither every day over Bifrost, which is also called Asa-bridge. There stands a beautiful hall near the fountain beneath the ash. Out of it come three maids. These maids shape the lives of men and we call them the Norns. On the boughs of the ash sits an eagle, who knows many things. Between his eyes sits the hawk, called Vedfolner. A squirrel, by name Ratatösk, springs up and down the tree and bears words of hate between the eagle and Nidhug. Four stags leap about in the branches of the ash and bite the buds. The Norns that dwell by the fountain of Urd every day take water from the fountain, and clay that lies around the fountain, and sprinkle therewith the ash, in order that its branches may not wither or decay. . . . In Valhal there is a chest, kept by Ithun, in which are the apples that the gods must bite when they grow old, in order to become young again."[1]

In the above description the various denizens of the tree have been supposed to symbolise natural phenomena. The stags who bite the buds are the four cardinal winds; the eagle and the hawk represent respectively the air and the wind-still ether; the serpent Nidhug who gnaws the root in the subterranean abyss symbolises volcanic forces, and the squirrel, who runs up and down the tree, hail and other atmospheric phenomena.

[1] *The Prose or Younger Edda*, translated by G. W. Dasent, p. 16.

A similar if somewhat less detailed symbolism is met with in both the Indian and Persian traditions of the world-tree, a symbolism which often obscures and overshadows its cosmic function. In both countries the mythical tree was venerated rather as a tree

FIG. 27.—Yggdrasil—the Scandinavian world-tree.
(From Finn Magnusen's *Eddalaeren*.)

of life, the source of the immortalising soma or haoma, than as the supporter of the universe. The latter function was not indeed quite lost sight of, for the Kalpadruma of the Vedas was a cloud-tree of colossal size, which grew on a steep mountain, and by its shadow produced day and night before the creation of the sun and moon; and in the Rig-Veda Brahma himself is described as the vast over-spreading tree of the universe, of which the gods are the branches. Similarly in Persian legend, near the haoma-tree stood the tree of all seeds, frequented by two birds, one of which when he settled on it broke off a thousand branches and caused their seeds to fall, while the other carried them to a place whence they might be conveyed to the earth with the rain. The same idea, even to the two birds, recurs in the Indian traditions of the mystical soma-tree, which, besides producing the immortalising drink, also bore fruit and seed of every kind. It was from this tree that the immortals shaped the heaven and the earth: it grew in the third heaven, overshadowing it with its branches. Beneath it sat the gods, quaffing the precious soma, whereby they preserved their immortality.

Amongst the followers of Buddha this tradition of a supernatural tree underwent a further process of idealisation. Their fancy described it as covered with divine flowers, and gleaming with every kind of precious stone. To its smallest leaf it was formed of gems. It grew on a pure and level sward, resplendent in colour as the peacock's neck. It received the homage of the gods.[1] It was beneath this tree that Gautama took his seat, resolved not to stir until he had attained to perfect knowledge. The tempter Mâra, with his hosts of demons, assailed him with fiery darts, with rain in floods and hurricanes; but the Buddha remained unmoved, until the defeated demons fled away. This is probably a Buddhist rendering of the Vedic account of the great fight between the powers of light and darkness for the clouds and the ambrosia they contained. Gautama also wins the

---

[1] De Gubernatis, *op. cit.* vol. i. p. 80.

victory, but for him it is knowledge and enlightenment that should constitute the true object of human desire.

Briefer references to the cosmic tree are met with in the traditions of other races. According to the Phoenicians the universe was framed on the model of a tent, its axis a revolving cosmic tree, supporting a blue canopy on which the heavenly bodies were embroidered. The Egyptians, in one of their schemes of the universe, also represented the central axis as a colossal tree, on whose branches Bennu the sun god perched. It gave forth celestial rain, which descended on the fields of Lower Egypt, and penetrated to the under-world to refresh those who are in Amenti. The Osirian Tât-pillar, alluded to in a previous chapter, is thought by Professor Tiele to be derived from the conception of the world-pillar, though M. Maspero regards its cosmic symbolism as a later accretion.

"On a post on which is graven a human countenance, and which is covered with gay clothing, stands the so-called Tât-pillar, entirely made up of superimposed capitals, one of which has a rude face scratched upon it, intended no doubt to represent the shining sun. On the top of the pillar is placed the complete head-dress of Osiris, the ram's horns, the sun, the ureus adder, the double feather, all emblems of light and sovereignty, which in my judgment must have been intended to represent the highest heaven."[1]

The conception of the world-tree is also found in the golden gem-bearing tree of the sky, where, according to Egyptian mythology, Núit had her abode. "She is goddess of the heavenly ocean, whose body is decked with stars. The pilgrim to the lower world

[1] C. P. Tiele, *History of the Egyptian Religion* (London, 1882), p. 46.

eats of the fruit, and the goddess leaning from the tree pours out the water of life." This was in the west on the way travelled by the dead. To the east there was another tree, with wide radiating branches bearing jewels, up which the strong morning sun, Horus, climbed to the zenith of heaven. It has been suggested that this "Sycamore of Emerald" was a mythological rendering of the beautiful green tints on the horizon at the rising and setting of the sun.[1]

The tradition of a universe-tree is found also in China and Japan. The legends of the latter country speak of an enormous metal pine which grows in the north at the centre of the world.[2] In Chinese mythology seven miraculous trees once flourished on the Kuen Lün Mountains. One of them, which was of jade, bore fruit that conferred immortality; another, named Tong, grew on the highest peak, "hard by the closed gate of heaven."[3]

It is interesting to find somewhat similar traditions current in the New World. According to the cosmogony of the Sia Indians — a small diminished tribe inhabiting New Mexico—there was in each of the six regions of the world, North, South, East, West, Zenith, and Nadir, a mountain bearing a giant tree, in a spring at the foot of which dwelt one of the six "cloud rulers," each attended by one of the six primal Sia priestesses, chosen by the arch-mother to intercede with the cloud rulers to send rain to the Sia. The six trees were specified as the spruce, pine, aspen, cedar, and two varieties of the oak.[4]

The beautiful conception met with in some of the

---

[1] Lethaby, *Architecture, Mysticism, and Myth* (London, 1892), p. 120.
[2] *Ibid.* p. 111.
[3] *Babylonian and Oriental Record* (June 1888), pp. 149-159.
[4] *Eleventh Annual Report of the Bureau of Ethnology* (Washington, 1894).

above traditions, by which the stars were compared at once to gems and to the fruits of a mighty tree, is frequently encountered in ancient literature. The Arabians represented the zodiac as a tree with twelve branches, of which the stars were the fruit, and a somewhat similar idea appears in the Apocalyptic tree of life, which "bare twelve manner of fruits, and yielded her fruit every month."[1] The Babylonian hero Gilgames, in his wanderings beyond the gates of ocean, came upon a forest, which

> To the forest of the trees of the gods in appearance was equal;
> Emeralds it carried as its fruit;
> The branch refuses not to support a canopy;
> Crystal they carried as shoots,
> Fruit they carry and to the sight it is glistening.[2]

The device of a golden tree hung with jewels, which is common throughout the East in all fine goldsmiths' work, and a good example of which was formerly one of the treasures of the palace of the Great Mogul at Agra,[3] was no doubt derived from the conception of a star-bearing world-tree. For it must be remembered that the ancients believed gems to be self-lustrous like the stars. Homer's palaces emitted a radiance like moonlight, and the columns of gold and emerald seen by Herodotus at Tyre gave out light.[4]

We have no direct instance of gem-bearing trees in Greek mythology, though the golden apples of the Hesperides growing on Mount Atlas, the sky-sustaining mountain in the country beyond the north wind, had evidently some kinship to the jewelled fruit of Eastern legend.

[1] Revelation xxii. 2.
[2] Lethaby, *op. cit.* p. 107.
[3] *Ibid.* p. 102.
[4] Herodotus, ii. 44.

In addition to the Norse Yggdrasil, there are other traces of the tradition of a world-tree to be met with amongst European nations. The Russians have a legend, derived from Byzantium, of an iron-tree, the root of which is the power of God, while its head sustains the three worlds, the heavenly ocean of air, the earth, and hell with its burning fire and brimstone.[1] Amongst the Saxons the idea of a world-tree seems to have persisted even to the time of Charlemagne, who in the course of his campaign against them in 772 A.D. solemnly destroyed as a heathen idol their Irmensûl or "World-pillar," a lofty tree-trunk, which they worshipped as typifying the universal column that supports all things. Mannhardt, however, regards the Irmensûl as simply a national tree, corresponding to the community trees already mentioned, and explains Charlemagne's act as a political rather than a religious one.[2]

In the Cathedral at Hildesheim there is an ancient stone column known as the Irmensäule (though its claim to the name is disputed), which was dug up under Louis le Débonnaire, and transformed into a candelabrum surmounted by an image of the Virgin,[3] the conception of moral support thus taking the place of the grosser idea of a material stay.

As in Eastern legend the universe-tree was venerated as something more than a mere material supporter of the world, being sometimes the giver of wisdom and sometimes the conveyer of immortality, so in European myth it is found linked with a similar beneficence. In the legends of the Finns its branches are represented as conferring "eternal welfare," and

---

[1] De Gubernatis, *op. cit.* vol. i. p. 102.
[2] Mannhardt I. 307.
[3] Goblet d'Alviella, *op. cit.* pp. 107, 113.

"the delight that never ceases." The Kalevala, which dates back to an unknown antiquity, relates how the last of created trees, the oak, sprang from the magic acorn planted by the hero Wainamoinen in the ashes of burnt hay which had been mown by the water-maidens :—

> Spreads the oak-tree many branches,
> Rounds itself a broad corona,
> Raises it above the storm clouds ;
> Far it stretches out its branches,
> Stops the white clouds in their courses,
> With its branches hides the sunlight,
> With its many leaves the moonbeams,
> And the starlight dies in heaven.

> Sad the lives of man and hero,
> Sad the house of ocean-dwellers,
> If the sun shines not upon them,
> If the moonlight does not cheer them.

At the prayer of Wainamoinen, appalled by the monstrous growth, his mother, the wind-spirit, sends a tiny water-creature, who, soon turning into a giant, with a mighty swing of his hatchet strikes the tree. With the second stroke he cuts it, and with the third fire springs from its huge bulk and the oak yields, "shaking earth and heaven in falling." It is not till then that its beneficent powers are made manifest :—

> Eastward far the trunk extending,
> Far to westward flew the tree-tops,
> To the south the leaves were scattered,
> To the north its hundred branches.
> Whosoe'er a branch has taken
> Has obtained eternal welfare.
> Who receives himself a tree top

> He has gained the master-magic.
> Who the foliage has gathered
> Has delight that never ceases.[1]

The corresponding legend amongst the neighbouring Esthonians, as told in their epic, the Kalevipoeg, contains a quaint medley of the practical and the poetic. Here, too, the monstrous oak is felled by a giant who grows from a dwarf; in falling it covers the sea with its branches and is quickly turned to use by the people. From the trunk is fashioned a bridge with two arms, one stretching to Finland, the other to an adjoining island. Ships are built from the crown, and towns from the roots, and toy-boats from the chips. What is left over is used to build shelters for old men, widows, and orphans, and the last remainder to provide a hut for the minstrel. Therewith he gains "the master-magic," for the strangers who cross the bridge now and again, and stop at his door to ask what city and what splendid palace stand before them, receive for answer that the palace is his poor hut, and all the splendour around is the light of his songs reflected from heaven.[2]

To return again to the East, it has already been mentioned that in a tradition common both to the Persians and the Hindus, and therefore presumably of considerable antiquity, the cosmic tree produced the food whereby the gods preserved their immortality. The universe-tree had become a tree of life. This conception of a mystical life-giving tree was associated with the ritual use of an earthly counterpart of the immortalising drink.

According to the Persian tradition the haoma-

---

[1] *Kalevala*, Second Rune.
[2] W. F. Kirby, *The Hero of Esthonia* (London, 1895), vol. i. p. 48.

tree grew beside the tree of all seeds in a lake, where it was guarded by two fish against the attacks of the lizard sent by Ahriman to destroy the sacred sap wherewith the gods were nourished. It was the first of all trees planted by Ormuzd in the fountain of life, and was identified with the god Haoma, who gave strength and health to the body, and to the soul enlightenment and eternal life. This god was regarded as assimilated to the earthly haoma, and as present in it. It is related in the sacred writings that he appeared one day to Zoroaster as he was tending the holy fire, and thus addressed him: " I am the divine Haoma, who keeps death at bay. Call upon me, express my juice that ye may enjoy me ; worship me with songs of praise." Zoroaster replied, " Honour to Haoma. He is good, well, and truly born, the giver of welfare and health, victorious and of golden hue ; his branches bow down that one may enjoy them. To the soul he is the way to heaven. In the beginning Ormuzd gave to Haoma the girdle glittering with stars, wherewith he girded himself upon the tops of the mountains."[1]

The juice of the terrestrial haoma was obtained from the plant by the use of pestle and mortar, and was taken whenever prayer was offered. Every house in Persia had its haoma-plant and its sacred pestle and mortar, which had to be protected from pollution as carefully as the holy fire and the sacred myrtle-twigs. The preparation of the haoma-drink had its special liturgy, and in dedicating it the cup was held aloft, not placed on the ground, lest it should be polluted by the breath of the worshipper or other impurity.[2] The Semnion or Theombrotion which, according to Pliny,

[1] Bötticher, *op. cit.* p. 516.   [2] *Ibid.* p. 518.

was taken by the Persian kings to keep off bodily decay and to produce constancy of mind, was probably identical with the haoma-drink.[1]

The Parsees of Bombay still continue the ritual use of the haoma-juice, deriving it from a plant with a knotted stem and leaves like those of the jasmine, supplies of which are specially obtained from Kirman in Persia. They refuse to admit the identity of the Vedic soma with their own sacred plant, which they assert is never found in India.[2]

This fact, if true, would account for the confusion which appears to exist as to the exact nature of the plant from which the Vedic soma or amrita was derived, and indeed it is very probable that in their migrations southward the Hindus made use successively of different plants. But there can be little doubt that the soma ritual and the conceptions associated with it were originally derived from the same source as that of the haoma, and date back to a period before the Aryan races had become separated. Like the haoma, the soma is not only a plant but also a powerful deity, and in both the Vedas and the Zendavesta "the conceptions of the god and the sacred juice blend wonderfully with each other."[3]

According to Professor Roth, the plant which is the source of the intoxicating drink offered to the gods in Hindu sacrifices is the *Sarcostemma acidum* or *Asclepias acida*, a leafless herb containing a milky juice, but it is doubtful whether it is identical with the Vedic soma plant.[4] Dr. Haug states distinctly that the plant at present used by the sacrificial priests of

---

[1] Pliny, xxiv. 102.
[2] Folkard, *op. cit.* p. 378.
[3] Windischmann, quoted by Herbert Spencer, *Principles of Sociology*, vol. i. p. 375.
[4] De Gubernatis, *op. cit.* vol. ii. p. 350.

the Deccan is not the soma of the Vedas. It grows on the hills near Poona; its sap, which is whitish, is bitter and astringent, but not sour; it is a very nasty drink, but has some intoxicating effect. De Gubernatis concludes that as the earthly drink was merely a symbol of the heavenly soma, its source and character were not material. It is not necessary that the drink which the worshipper pretends to drink or to offer to Indra at the sacrifice should be really intoxicating. The object of the rite is to induce Indra in heaven to drink the water of strength, the true soma, the real ambrosia, sometimes conceived as hidden in the clouds, sometimes as dwelling in the soft light poured forth by the great Soma, Indu, the moon,—the tree whose stem, long, dark, and leafless, resembles that of the earthly plant from which the drink is ordered to be prepared. The ritual resolves itself, according to De Gubernatis, into a sun-charm. Soma, the moon, the god of plants, the lord of the dark forest of night or winter, is the good genius who furnishes the miraculous drink wherewith Indra, the solar hero, recruits his forces. It is under its influence, say the Vedas, that Indra performs his great deeds. Soma does really intoxicate the gods in heaven, incessantly renewing the triumph of light over its enemies. The sacrifice of the soma on earth is only a pale, naïve, and grotesque reproduction of that divine miracle.[1]

According to the Vedas, however, the soma-drink, which Windischman describes as "the holiest offering of the ancient Indian worship," had a genuinely intoxicating effect. It is described as "stimulating speech," "calling forth the ardent thought," "generating hymns with the powers of a poet"; and is invoked as

[1] De Gubernatis, *op. cit.* vol. ii. p. 351.

"bestower of good, master of a thousand songs, the leader of sages." A hymn in the Rig-Veda has been thus translated:—

> We've quaffed the Soma bright
> And are immortal grown,
> We've entered into light
> And all the gods have known.
> What mortal now can harm
> Or foeman vex us more?
> Through thee, beyond alarm,
> Immortal god! we soar.[1]

In the Hindu worship the fermented juice of the soma-plant was presented in ladles to the deities invoked, part sprinkled on the sacrificial fire, part on the sacred grass strewed upon the floor, and the remainder invariably drunk by those who conducted the ceremony.[2] In early times, says Windischman, its use was looked upon as a holy action, and as a sacrament by which the union with Brahma was obtained.

The *ambrosia* of the Olympian gods, like the word itself, was no doubt in its essence identical with the Vedic *amrita* or *soma*. It contained the principle of immortality, and was hence withheld from mortals. But the word was also applied, like the soma, to a mixture of various fruits used in religious rites.[3] A still closer analogy, however, with the Hindu and Persian conception is to be found in the cult of Dionysus, who was regarded as present in the wine, which was his gift to man. "He, born a god," says Euripides, "is poured out in libations to the gods."[4] And again, "This god is a prophet. For when he forces his way into the body, he makes those who

---

[1] J. Muir, *Metrical Translations from Sanskrit writers* (London, 1879), p. 168.
[2] Folkard, *op. cit.* p. 548.
[3] Athenaeus, 473 C.
[4] *Bacchae*, 284.

rave to foretell the future."¹ The fact that Dionysus was essentially a tree-god, "the spiritual form of the vine,"² renders the analogy still more striking.

To discuss the genesis of the above conceptions would be to reopen the whole question of the origin of tree-worship. The drinking of vegetable juices, fermented or otherwise, was no doubt one of the means by which early races were accustomed to produce dreams and visions, and so, in their view, to get themselves possessed by or put into communication with a spirit. It was natural, therefore, for them to assume that the spirit in question had entered into them with the drug, and was therefore present in it and in the plant from which it was derived. Mr. Herbert Spencer, indeed, argues that this particular assumption was one of the chief factors in the origin of plant-worship in general, a main reason why plants yielding intoxicating agents, and hence other plants, came to be regarded as containing supernatural beings.³ It would probably, however, be safer to conclude that the sacramental use of the juice of plants is merely one amongst many cognate religious usages, and like the ritual employment of wreaths in the service of the gods, the attachment of branches to the house, and the smiting with the "life-rood," sprang out of the desire of men to bring nearer to themselves a spirit already believed to exist, and thus to ensure their enjoyment of the protection and the benefits presumed to be at his disposal.

¹ *Bacchae*, 297.
² W. Pater, *Greek Studies* (London, 1895), p. 7.
³ *Principles of Sociology*, vol. i. p. 377.

CHAPTER VII

PARADISE

No account of tree-worship would be complete without a chapter on that tradition of a paradise or ideal garden of delight which is met with in the mythology of almost all the nations of antiquity. The form of the tradition varies. Paradise was sometimes represented (1) as the seat of the gods; sometimes (2) as the first home of the parents of mankind; and in other cases as (3) the abode of the spirits of the blessed. Occasionally the different conceptions are combined; but the earlier traditions all concur in connecting paradise with a miraculous tree or trees, or with a more or less legendary mountain, from which it may be plausibly inferred that they date back to the days of that primitive cosmogony when the heavens were supposed to be upheld by a material support. Thus in one, at least, of its aspects the tradition of paradise must be regarded as an offshoot of the sacred tree.

It is not difficult to understand how the various conceptions arose. In the first place, as the idea of a life or spirit more or less bound to the tree became expanded into that of a powerful and wide-ranging god, the idealising process demanded for him some home in heaven corresponding to the tree which was his favourite habitat or embodiment on earth. The sacred god-haunted tree, to which worship and gifts were accorded below, suggested a mystical counterpart above, and the proper home of deity was assumed to be that marvellous tree whose branches were the sky and its fruit the sun and stars, or that lofty mountain whose summit touched and supported the heavens.

In the second place, the belief, common in primitive mythology, that the first parents were born from trees, presumably led to the idea that these honoured ancestors, whose innocence was a part of their idealisation, lived amongst trees and in a garden equally idealised.

The third conception of paradise naturally grew out of the earlier conceptions, when there arose the belief in a future life of reward or punishment; though it has been pointed out that the conception of heaven under the form of a garden prevailed, *par excellence*, amongst settled nations, living under kings of whose state a luxurious garden or pleasaunce formed an essential part.[1]

Of paradise regarded as the abode of the gods, the Indian tradition of the garden of Indra furnishes the best example. It was situated on Mount Meru, on the confines of Cashmere, and contained the five wonderful trees which sprang from the waters, after the churning of the cosmic ocean by the gods and the demons. Under these trees the gods took their ease, enjoying the ambrosia that fell from them. The garden, watered by springs and rivulets, contained luminous flowers, fruits that conferred immortality, and birds whose song even the gods loved to hear.

[1] De Gubernatis, *op. cit.* vol. i. p. 261.

The chief of its five miraculous trees was the paridjata, the flower of which preserved its freshness throughout the year, contained in itself every scent and flavour, and gave happiness to whoever demanded it. It was, moreover, a test of virtue, losing its splendour in the hands of the sinful, and preserving it for him who followed duty. Each person found in it his favourite colour and perfume. It served as a torch by night, was a talisman against hunger, thirst, disease, and decrepitude, and discoursed the sweetest and most varied music.[1] De Gubernatis quotes several other instances from Indian literature of a legendary celestial garden.[2]

Of paradise, as the home of the first parents, the Pentateuch gives the most circumstantial account, though it would appear from Genesis iii. 8 that the Biblical paradise was also regarded as a favourite resort of Jehovah. The sacred books of the Parsis contain a very similar version. The original human pair, Maschia and Maschiâna, sprang from a tree in Heden, a delightful spot where grew hom or haoma, the marvellous tree of life, whose fruit imparted vigour and immortality. The woman, at the instance of Ahriman, the spirit of evil in the guise of a serpent, gave her husband fruit to eat and so led to their ruin.[3]

FIG. 28.—From a Babylonian seal.
(Goblet d'Alviella.)

The tradition is no doubt of very ancient origin, and is supposed to be represented on an early Babylonian

---

[1] De Gubernatis, vol. i. p. 262. [2] *Ibid.* p. 182.
[3] Folkard, *op. cit.* p. 9.

seal now in the British Museum. The tree stands in the middle, from either side two human beings seated stretch forth their hands for its fruit; the serpent stands erect behind one of them.[1] On another cylinder in the Museum at the Hague there is represented a garden with trees and birds; in the middle a palm, from which two personages are plucking the fruit; a third with a fruit in his hand seems to address them.[2]

The two mystical trees of the Biblical paradise find their common counterpart in the sacred cedar of the Chaldaeans, which, besides being essentially a tree of life, employed in magic rites to restore strength and life to the body, was also "the revealer of the oracles of earth and heaven." Upon its core the name of Ea, the god of wisdom, was supposed to be written,[3] just as the name of Ormuzd was first disclosed to man by appearing carved in the wood of his sacred cypress. The tree of life also finds a parallel in the divine soma, the giver of eternal youth and immortality, a drink reserved only for the celestial gods or the souls of the blessed.

The third conception of paradise, as the dwelling-place of the righteous dead, is met with in the earliest Greek literature,[4] but there is no definite trace of it amongst the Semitic nations until much later. It did not, apparently, find recognition amongst the Jews until after the exile, but references to it are frequent in their later apocalyptic literature.[5] In the second book of Esdras, the Lord tells His people that He will bring them out of the tombs, and that He has sancti-

---

[1] G. Smith, *Chaldaean Account of Genesis*, pp. 88, 89.
[2] J. Menant, *op. cit.* vol. i. fig. 121.
[3] Sayce, *op. cit.* p. 240.
[4] Homer, *Odyssey*, iv. 563; Hesiod, *Works and Days*, 166.
[5] *Encyclop. Brit.*, 9th edition, vol. viii. p. 536.

fied and prepared for them "twelve trees, laden with divers fruits, and as many fountains flowing with milk and honey, and seven mighty mountains, whereupon there grow roses and lilies."[1] "They shall have the tree of life for an ointment of sweet savour; they shall neither labour nor be weary."[2]

In the Rabbinical writings, and still more in the Koran, this conception of paradise is embroidered with many fanciful extravagances. The Talmud even invents two paradises. "There is an upper paradise and a lower paradise. And between them is fixed a pillar, by which they are joined together, and which is called 'The strength of the Hill of Sion.' And by this pillar on every Sabbath and festival the souls of the righteous ascend from the lower to the upper paradise, and there enjoy the light of the Divine Majesty till the end of the Sabbath or festival, when they descend and return into the lower paradise."[3]

This pillar is no doubt a survival of the old tradition of the world-tree, a tradition still more obviously traceable in the Mahometan belief. According to the Koran paradise is situated in the seventh heaven. In the centre of it stands the marvellous tree called *Tooba*, which is so large that a man mounted on the fleetest horse could not ride round its branches in a hundred years. This tree not only affords the most grateful shade over the whole extent of the Mussulman paradise, but its boughs, laden with delicious fruits of a size and taste unknown to mortals, bend themselves to be plucked at the wish of the happy denizens of that blissful abode. The rivers of paradise take their rise from the tree, flowing some with water,

---

[1] 2 Esdras ii. 18.
[2] *Ibid.* ii. 12.
[3] Eisenmenger, *Entdecktes Judenthum* (1700), Bd. II. p. 318.

some with milk, and some with honey; while others are filled with wine, the use of which is not forbidden to the blessed.[1]

The confusion of thought apparent in these ancient traditions of paradise was no doubt partly due to the fact that primitive man, with his limited grasp of the possibilities of space, pictured heaven as not far distant from him. It was a happier and a brighter earth, which offered material rather than spiritual joys, and where, according to the earliest conceptions, the spirits of the departed carried on the same pursuits, reaped and sowed and hunted, as they had done while in life. Thus the old Accadian dwellers by the Euphrates pictured the sky as the counterpart of their own fertile plains, and the sun as a ploughman yoking his oxen to the glittering plough, with which he tilled the heavenly pasture.[2] The same idea is exemplified in the names of the zodiacal constellations, which are of extremely ancient origin, the sign we still know as Taurus being called by the Accadians "the bull who guides the year." So near was heaven that it was not impossible to climb up to it, if you could but find the cosmic tree by which it was upheld. The Khasias of India have a legend that the stars are men who have climbed into heaven by a tree.[3] The Mbocobis of Paraguay still believe that the souls of the dead go up "to the earth on high" by the tree which joins us to heaven, and find an entrance by means of the holes in the sky-roof through which the rain descends.[4] There is a Chinese story of a king, who having heard of the glories of paradise, set forth in search of it. After long wanderings he came to a mighty column, which,

[1] Folkard, *op. cit.* p. 10.
[2] A. H. Sayce, *op. cit.* p. 48.
[3] Goblet d'Alviella, *op. cit.* p. 171.
[4] E. B. Tylor, *Early History of Mankind* (London, 1878), p. 358.

he had been told, must be climbed in order to reach the wished-for goal. But it was too slippery, and he was compelled to fall back upon the alternative route, a steep and rugged mountain path. When almost fainting with fatigue he was assisted by some friendly nymphs, and at length arrived at a beautiful garden, with a wondrous tree in its midst, and a fountain of immortality, from which four rivers, flowing to the four corners of the earth, took their rise.[1]

The same notion of the similarity and propinquity of the heavenly field is illustrated by the story of the Etruscan priest, who by his charms brought down to earth a bit of heaven whereon to build his temple. The Mahometans assert that the Caaba was lowered directly from the celestial paradise exactly at the centre of the earth. And the Bedouins of Arabia still believe that the jinni, living near the lowest heaven, can hear the conversation of the angels, and so gain valuable information which they are able to impart to men.[2]

Homer placed the seat of the gods and the court of Zeus upon the summit of Olympus,[3] which was supposed to touch heaven, and piercing through the region of rain and cloud to reach into the calm ether, where reigned eternal spring. By later writers, however, Olympus was represented as an unsubstantial region overhead, with the palace of Zeus in its midst. The earlier view of Olympus exactly corresponds with the Chaldaean "mount of the world," the mountain of Arallu or Hades, where the gods had their seat, and beneath which was the world of ghosts;[4] also with the Mount of the Assembly spoken of by Isaiah, and with

[1] W. F. Warren, *Paradise Found* (London, 1885), p. 144.
[2] J. Theodore Bent, *Nineteenth Century* (October 1895), p. 607.
[3] *Iliad*, xi. 76.
[4] Sayce, *op. cit.* p. 360.

the Scandinavian Asgard. But there is a clearer reminiscence of the elevated paradise of Oriental legend in the beautiful gardens of the world-supporting Atlas, with their delicious fruits, their golden apples, and their protecting dragon. The third conception of paradise, as the abode of the blessed, is also met with in Greek mythology in the Elysian fields, or islands of the blessed, also placed by some authorities in the neighbourhood of Mount Atlas. Here the souls of the virtuous enjoyed perfect happiness, in bowers for ever green, and amongst meadows watered by pleasant streams and bestarred with asphodel. The air was pure and serene, the birds warbled in the groves, and the inhabitants carried on such avocations as they had delighted in when on earth. Later writers, however, substituted for these innocent pleasures the voluptuous indulgences of the Mahometan paradise.

It was, no doubt, the ancient tradition of an elevated paradise, of a paradise seated on the summit of a heaven-touching world-mountain, which influenced Milton in his celebrated description, for there is nothing in the Biblical account to suggest the excessive altitude that he so deliberately accentuates. Paradise, according to the poet—

>   crowns with her enclosure green,
> As with a rural mound, the champain head
> Of a steep wilderness, . . .
>   and overhead up-grew
> Insuperable height of loftiest shade,
> Cedar, and pine, and fir, and branching palm;
>   . . . Yet higher than their tops
> The verdurous wall of paradise up-sprung.
>
> And higher than that wall a circling row
> Of goodliest trees, loaden with fairest fruit.[1]

---

[1] *Paradise Lost*, Book IV. 133-147.

As man's conceptions of God have widened with a more extended knowledge of His universe and a fuller realisation of his own history on the earth, these older conceptions of paradise as the home of deity and the abode of the blessed have decayed, until at the present day, however much our theologians may differ in their descriptions of heaven, they agree at least in this, that whatever it is, it is not a garden. But the belief in the existence of an earthly paradise, which formed a part of the traditions of so many ancient nations, lingered on for centuries after "the Holy City" of the New Testament had displaced the Paradise of the Old.

The features of this earthly paradise are for the most part similar to those familiar to us in the Biblical description. It contained the fountain of immortality, from which sprang the four rivers that flowed to the four quarters of the earth. Purling brooks ran with the far-famed ambrosia. The dwellers therein reposed on flowery lawns, lulled by the melodious warblings of birds and feasting on delicious fruits. Whatever there was of beautiful or sublime in nature there found its more perfect counterpart. Absolute contentment and serenity and the delight that never dies were the boons it offered. There man could cease from toil, for nature, unassisted, produced all that was necessary for his sustenance. This garden of delight was often sought after but seldom found, except by semi-divine heroes divinely led. Hercules, directed by Nereus, the sea-god, succeeded in attaining the gardens of the Hesperides on the world-supporting Mount Atlas, the Pillar of Heaven, as Herodotus calls it. He conquered the protecting dragon and secured the golden sun-fruit from the central tree.[1] The Chaldaean

---

[1] Hesiod, *Theogn.* 215 *et seq.*

Hercules, Gilgames, referred to in a previous chapter, found a similar tree with magic fruit upon it when he reached the gates of ocean.

This idea of an actual paradise upon earth has fascinated the mind of man in all ages, and has been one of his most cherished and persistent traditions. It was an idea that no doubt arose out of and corresponded to his lifelong craving for a perfect peace and happiness which he never found in the world he knew, and which he has at length realised to be incompatible with his own organisation. It has taken him centuries to discover that if there is no earthly paradise it is he himself and not the world that is at fault. But the tradition was slow to die, and there are probably people who still believe, as Sir John Maundeville believed in the fourteenth century, that the Garden of Eden exists somewhere upon the earth if it could only be found. This is what the famous traveller says :—

"And beyond the land, and isles, and deserts of Prester John's lordship, in going straight towards the East, men find nothing but mountains and great rocks ; and there is the dark region, where no man may see, neither by day nor night, as they of the country say. And that desert, and that place of darkness, lasts from this coast unto Terrestrial Paradise, where Adam, our first father, and Eve were put, who dwelt there but a little while, and that is towards the east, at the beginning of the earth.

"Of Paradise I cannot properly speak, for I was not there. It is far beyond ; and I repent not going there, but I was not worthy. But as I have heard say of wise men beyond, I shall tell you with good-will. Terrestrial Paradise, as wise men say, is the highest place of the earth ; and it is so high that it nearly touches the circle of the moon, there as the moon makes her turn. For it is so high that the flood of Noah might not come to it, that would have covered all the earth of the world all about, and above and beneath, except Paradise. And this Paradise is enclosed all about with a wall, and men know not whereof it is; for the wall is covered all over with moss, as it seems; and it seems not that the wall is natural stone. And that wall stretches from the south to the north; and it has but one entry, which is closed with burning fire, so that no man that is mortal dare enter. And in the highest place of Paradise, exactly in the middle, is a well that casts out four streams, which run by divers lands, of which the first is called Pison or Ganges, that runs through India or Emlak, in which river are many precious stones, and much lignum aloës, and much sand of gold. And the other river is called Nile or Gyson, which goes through Ethiopia, and after through Egypt. And the other is called Tigris, which runs by Assyria and by Armenia the Great. And the other is called Euphrates, which runs through Media, Armenia, and Persia. And men there beyond say that all the sweet waters of the world, above and beneath, take their beginning from the well of Paradise; and out of that well all waters come and go."[1]

The paradise in the existence of which the great traveller so firmly believed is represented in a thirteenth-century map as a circular island lying to the east of India, and the cartographer has not forgotten to introduce even the gate from which our first parents were expelled.

A fourteenth-century Icelandic saga describes a

[1] *Early Travels in Palestine* (London, Bohn, 1848), p. 276.

voyage undertaken by a prince and his chosen friend in search of the Deathless Land. They first went to Constantinople to consult the Emperor, and were told that the earthly paradise was slightly to the south of India. Arrived in that country they continued the journey on horseback, and came at last to a dense forest, the gloom of which was so great through the interlacing of the boughs that even by day the stars could be seen. Emerging from it they saw, across a strait, a beautiful land, which was unmistakably paradise. The strait was crossed by a stone bridge guarded by a dragon. The prince, in no ways deterred, walked deliberately sword in hand against the dragon, and the next moment, to his infinite surprise and delight, he found himself in paradise. Here he encountered all the joys heart could desire, and exhausted with delight he fell asleep. In his dreams his guardian angel appeared to him and promised to lead him home, but to come for him again and take him away for ever at the expiration of the tenth year.[1]

Many other mediaeval stories could be quoted, in which the traveller claims to have found paradise. It was a favourite subject with the court minstrels, proving that even the envied dwellers around a throne are not less open than other men to the fascinating dream of a still more perfect happiness.

Plato's story of the lost Atlantis, supposed to have been related to Solon when in Egypt, also belongs to the class of paradise legends. It was situated in the Atlantic, in the neighbourhood of the Pillars of Hercules. Larger than Libya and Asia together, it was the seat of a great and wonderful empire, the subjects of which, after many conquests, set out to subdue Hellas, but

[1] S. Baring-Gould, *Curious Myths of the Middle Ages* (London, 1866), p. 236.

were defeated by the Athenians. Shortly afterwards there arose violent earthquakes and floods, and in a single day and night the island disappeared beneath the sea. All this happened 9000 years before the time of Plato.[1] According to other accounts, when the gods distributed the whole earth amongst themselves Atlantis fell to the lot of Poseidon, and the children he had by Cleito, a mortal, ruled over the surrounding country. The eldest, Atlas, gave his name to the island and to the Atlantic Ocean. This sacred land brought forth in abundance the most beautiful and delicious fruits, and magnificent buildings were constructed from the minerals and fragrant woods of the place, notably a holy temple dedicated to Poseidon and Cleito, which was protected by an enclosure of gold. A wealth of fountains and hot and cold springs supplied luxurious baths. The government was humane and just, and the people took their due share in it. So long as the divine nature lasted in them they were obedient to the laws and well affected to the gods, their kinsmen, evincing gentleness and wisdom in the various chances of life and in their intercourse with each other, and setting more value on virtue than on wealth and luxury. But in the end, as the divine part in them died away, they fell from virtue, and they and their island were submerged for ever beneath the waves.

This legend, which would appear to combine with the idea of an earthly paradise another tradition equally familiar to antiquity, that of a retributory deluge, survived into the Middle Ages, and became blended with the legends of the Celtic Church. For the Atlantic paradise is distinctly reproduced in that legendary Isle of Avalon,[2] which St. Brandan, an Irish saint of

---

[1] Plato, *Timaeus*, iii.   [2] W. F. Warren, *op. cit.* p. 12.

the sixth century, was said to have found in the course of a seven years' voyage; the isle—

> Where falls not hail or rain or any snow,
> Nor ever wind blows loudly, but it lies
> Deep-meadowed, happy, fair, with orchard lawns
> And bowery hollows.

Columbus, in his third voyage, came upon a spot, the site of which corresponded with the description given of the earthly paradise by "holy and wise theologians." But he hesitated to *ascend* thither and assure himself of the correctness of his conclusion, as no one could succeed in such an undertaking without the divine permission.[1]

The Japanese have a legend of an Island of Eternal Youth, which exists beyond the horizon in the shadowy unknown. Some fortunate observers have from time to time seen a wondrous tree rising high above the waves. It is the tree which has stood for all ages on the loftiest peak of Fusan, the Mountain of Immortality. The island has the traditional characteristics of the earthly paradise,—endless spring, airs ever sweet, unclouded skies, unfading flowers, birds that sing of love and joy, trees whose celestial dews carry with them the secret of eternity. Sorrow, pain, and death are unknown, and the elect of the gods, who people that delightful spot, fill their days with music and laughter and song, knowing nothing of the flight of time. The miracle of the spring in other lands is due to the whisper of the spirit of the island.[2]

This Japanese legend preserves the intimate connection between paradise and the cosmic tree, which is often found to have dropped out of other versions of

---
[1] *Select Letters of Columbus* (Hakluyt Society), p. 137.
[2] *Old-World Japan*, p. 79.

the tradition. There can be no doubt, however, that originally the mystical tree was the essential feature of paradise, and the garden was merely its precinct or setting—one of the many conceptions which grew up around the central idea of the cosmic tree. Each nation, according to its stage of culture or its prevailing habit of thought, emphasised one feature of it. The monster tree which, according to primitive cosmogony, was believed to support the universe by material branches, became in the minds of more cultivated races the central tree of a dimly-realised paradise, and eventually the symbol of an abstract idea. The intellectual Buddhist saw in it the emblem of knowledge; the Persian thought of it as the tree of immortality; the Hebrew, filled with the idea of man's frailty and with the longing to explain it, made it the tree of temptation.[1]

But in all these various conceptions we find a central idea, derived no doubt from an antecedent and universal tree-worship, an idea which places a tree at the root of all philosophy, refers all phenomena to the existence of a central tree, serviceable to man here or hereafter, and concentrating upon itself the reverent devotion which had outgrown its earthly counterpart.

There are many facts to prove the importance attached in ancient times to this conception of a glorified tree. Amongst the gorgeous decorations of the palaces of Eastern kings a symbolical representation of the tree of paradise was frequently found.

> Tall as the cedar of the mountain, here
> Rose the gold branches, hung with emerald leaves,
> Blossomed with pearls, and rich with ruby fruit.

---

[1] Goblet d'Alviella, *op. cit.* p. 176.

Sir John Maundeville describes one which he saw in the palace of the Chan of Cathay. "It is a vine made of fine gold, which spreads all about the hall, and it has many clusters of grapes, some white, some green, some yellow, some red, and some black, all of precious stones; the white are of crystal, beryl, and iris; the yellow of topazes; the red of rubies, grenaz, and alabraundines; the green of emeralds and perydoz and of chrysolites; and the black of onyx and garnets. And they are all so properly made that it appears a real vine, bearing natural grapes."[1]

According to an Arab writer, quoted by Gibbon,[2] there existed in the magnificent palace of the Caliph of Bagdad, in 917 A.D., amongst other spectacles of rare and stupendous luxury, a tree of gold and silver, spreading into eighteen large branches, on which and on the lesser boughs sat a variety of birds made of the same precious metals. While the machinery effected spontaneous motions the several birds warbled their natural harmony. The intention was, no doubt, to represent the traditional luxuriance of paradise, and a similar motive is met with in Eastern design even in the present day.

The tradition of a king who built a false paradise, like Sheddad in Southey's *Thalaba*, seems always to have been current in Western Asia. There is in the British Museum a sculpture from Koyunjik representing a palace, or may be a temple, constructed in imitation of a paradise. The artificial hill, representing the world-mountain on which it stands, is planted with trees and flowers, and watered by a stream that issues from a hanging garden.

---

[1] Lethaby, *op. cit.* p. 97. [2] *Decline and Fall*, chap. lii.

CHAPTER VIII

MAY CELEBRATIONS

IN these days, when so much is done to equalise the seasons, when in the flower-shops spring treads on the heels of autumn, and Christmas windows are gay with tropical fruits, when fresh meat is always on the stalls, and the earth is tapped of its light and warmth to make up for the absent sun, it is difficult to realise the delight and enthusiasm with which our forefathers welcomed the yearly miracle of the spring. It meant so much to them,—release from the cold and the darkness that fell hardly on all but the rich; a feast of colour to eyes weary of winter grays; luscious, varied, and plentiful food to palates dulled by salt meat and pease-pudding. No wonder that the first hint of the sun's return at Christmas, and the fulfilment of the promise of spring at May-day, were welcomed with an abandonment of joy to which our modern festivals offer but a pale parallel. It is doubtful, however, whether, even in the far-off days when the ceremonies possessed the highest religious sanction and significance, they were celebrated with a finer exuberance than in the comparatively recent times when this country was still "merrie England." Fetching in the May or going a-Maying was then a most important festival, in which people of all ranks took part. Henry VIII. himself rode a-Maying with Queen Katharine and his Court. Every village had its May-pole, and the first of May was everywhere "the maddest, merriest day of all the glad New Year." The celebration was recognised by the Roman Church, the note for the 30th of April in an old Calendar being, "The boys go out and seek May-trees."[1] Chaucer represents the whole Court as going into the fields "on May-day when the lark begins to rise"—

> To fetch the floures fresh and branch and blome.
> And namely hawthorne brought both page and grome,
> With freshë garlants party blew and white,
> And than rejoysen in their great delight.[2]

The poet makes the whole Court pelt each other with flowers, "the primerose, the violete and the gold," but the general custom was to bring home the branches and flowers as an adornment for the house. Even the barns and the cow-byres were carefully decorated, long after the primitive intention of the ceremony had been forgotten, and it had degenerated into a licensed opportunity for revelry and love-making.

The two aspects of the celebration, the decorative and the amatory, are charmingly illustrated in this lyric of Herrick's :—

> Come, my Corinna, come ; and coming mark
> How each field turns a street, each street a park,
>   Made green and trimmed with trees : see how
>   Devotion gives each house a bough
>   Or branch : each porch, each door ere this
>   An ark, a tabernacle is,
> Made up of white-thorn neatly interwove,
> As if here were those cooler shades of love.
> Can such delights be in the street
>   And open fields and we not see't?

---

[1] Brand's *Antiquities*, vol. i. p. 217.   [2] Court of Love, vv. 1431-35.

> Come, we'll abroad; and let's obey
> The proclamation made for May:
> And sin no more, as we have done by staying;
> But, my Corinna, come, let's go a-Maying.

The lover of old customs owes little to the Puritans, for they did their best to root them out, but he is certainly indebted to them incidentally for some valuable evidence as to those same customs, not otherwise attainable. Stubbs, a Puritan writer of the time of Elizabeth, thus describes the setting up of the Maypole in his time:—" But their cheefest jewell they bring from thence (the woods) in their Maie Poole, whiche they bring home with greate veneration as thus: They have twentie or fourtie yoke of oxen, every oxe havyng a sweete nosegaie of flowers tyed on the tippe of his hornes, and these oxen drawe home this Maie poole (this stinckyng idoll rather) which is covered all over with flowers and hearbes, bounde rounde aboute with stringes, from top to bottome, and sometimes painted with variable colours, with twoo or three hundred men, women, and children followyng it with greate devotion. And thus beyng reared up with handkercheifes and flagges streamyng on the toppe, they strawe the grounde aboute, binde greene boughes about it, sett up sommer-haules, bowers, and arbours hard by it. And then fall they to banquet and feast, to leape and daunce aboute it, as the Heathen people did at the dedication of their idolles, whereof this is a perfect patterne, or rather the thyng itself."[1]

"What adoe make our yong men at the time of May?" cries another Puritan writer. "Do they not use night-watchings to rob and steale young trees out of other men's grounde, and bring them home into

---

[1] *Anatomie of Abuses* (1585), p. 94.

their parishe, with minstrels playing before : and when they have set it up they will decke it with floures and garlands and daunce rounde (men and women togither, moste unseemley and intolerable, as I have proved before) about the tree, like unto the children of Israell that daunced about the golden calfe that they had set up." [1]

Thomas Hall, another author of the same class, was also moved to eloquence on the subject : " Had this rudeness been acted only in some ignorant and obscure parts of the land I had been silent ; but when I perceived that the complaints were general from all parts of the land, and that even in Cheapside itself the rude rabble had set up this ensign of profaneness, and had put the Lord Mayor to the trouble of seeing it pulled down, I could not, out of my dearest respects and tender compassion to the land of my nativity, and for the prevention of like disorders (if possible) for the future, but put pen to paper, and discover the sinful use and vile profaneness that attend such misrule." [2]

As every one knows, the Puritans had their will of the May-poles, and the Long Parliament in April 1644 decreed their removal as "a heathenish vanity, generally abused to superstition and wickednesse." They were indeed reinstated after the Restoration and the old festivities revived, but the Puritan epoch had left its mark upon the spirit of the people, and May-day was never again quite what it had been, so that the following lament by a writer of Cromwell's time was not quite out of date even when King Charles had again come to his own :—

[1] J. Northbrooke, *Treatise wherein Dicing, Daunceing, etc., are Reproved* (1577), p. 140.
[2] Brand's *Antiquities*, vol. i. p. 244.

Happy the age and harmlesse were the dayes
(For then true love and amity was found)
When every village did a May-pole raise,
And Whitsun-ales and May-games did abound,
And all the lusty yonkers in a rout
With merry lasses daunc'd the rod about.
Then Friendship to their banquets bid the guests
And poor men far'd the better for their feasts.
. . . .
But since the Summer poles were overthrown,
And all good sports and merriments decayed,
How times and men are chang'd so well is knowne,
It were but labour lost if more were said.

In England the once universal joy-making on the first of May has dwindled into a mere eleemosynary device, and every year takes away something even from this poor survival. We are only reminded of the day in London by here and there a peripatetic Jack-in-the-Green with his retinue of begging clowns, by the gay ribbons on a few draught horses, and by the newspaper reports of the election of Mr. Ruskin's May-queen at Whitelands College. But in many old-world towns and villages throughout the country the children still carry round wands, with bunches of flowers tied to them, or garlands, consisting of a little bower fashioned out of two crossed hoops, hidden in flowers, with a doll seated in the centre. The obvious intention of this pretty custom is the collection of coppers, which no one will grudge. It is, so to say, a religious ceremony, whereof only the collection has survived, as the following old rhyme sufficiently illustrates :—

Gentlemen and ladies !
We wish you happy May ;
We've come to show our garlands,
Because it is May-day ;
Come, kiss my face, and smell my mace,
And give the lord and lady something.[1]

---

[1] *Notes and Queries*, 3rd ser. vol. vii. p. 425.

In place of the final couplet it was sometimes the custom of one of the bearers to say, " Please to handsel the lord and lady's purse."

The practice once current in the North of England of going into the woods on the first of May, "when the day begins to break," and bringing home "knots of flowers and buds and garlands gay" wherewith to adorn the windows and doors of the houses at sunrise, is illustrated in the following doggrel, which used to be sung in the streets of Newcastle-on-Tyne:[1]—

> Rise up, maidens, fie for shame !
> For I've been four long miles from hame ;
> I've been gathering my garland gay,
> Rise up, fair maids, and take in your May.

It now remains to trace back these ceremonies— these survivals—to their origin, and to show how once they were the essential outcome of a living creed, and had a serious, and, so to speak, sacramental significance.[2] The May-day celebrations combined three different usages. *First*, the bringing in of the May and the decoration of the homestead. *Secondly*, the planting of the May-pole and the dancing around it. *Thirdly*, the selection of some youth or maiden as King or Queen of the May.

(1) The custom of going to the woods to fetch in the May is not by any means peculiar to England. It was until recently very general throughout Europe, and still survives in many districts, though sometimes Whitsuntide or Midsummer is the date chosen for the ceremony. This wide distribution at once stamps it as an ancient observance, and indeed it was already represented as such so long ago as the thirteenth

---

[1] Brand's *Antiquities*, vol. i. p. 219.   [2] Mannhardt I. p. 315.

century.¹ In some districts the branches that were brought in were fastened over the house door or upon the roof, or planted in front of the cattle stalls, a separate bush being attached for each head of cattle. Here the acknowledged purpose was to make the cows good milkers. "They fancy," says a writer on the manners of the Irish, "that a green bough fastened on May-day against the house will produce plenty of milk that summer."² In other districts the May-bushes were decorated with nosegays and ribbons and carried in solemn procession from house to house, the bearers singing a song and collecting their recompense in a basket. In some parts of Sweden on May-day eve boys still go round at the heels of the village fiddler, each with a bunch of freshly-gathered birch-twigs, singing songs in which fine weather, good harvests, and other blessings are entreated. At every cottage where they are duly compensated for their pains they adorn the door with one of their birch-sprays. In Stockholm on St. John's eve miniature May-poles, known as Majstänger, are sold by the thousand.³ In Russia the custom of decking the houses with branches at Whitsuntide is universal.⁴ Similar instances might be multiplied indefinitely.

Much light has been thrown on these May-day ceremonies by the study of many cognate observances met with amongst different nations and at different periods. In Western Germany and over the greater part of France it is customary at harvest-time to select a green sapling or branch, adorn it with flowers, ribbons, and coloured paper, and hang it with harvest fruits, eggs, cakes, and sweetmeats, and sometimes

---

[1] Mannhardt I. p. 160.
[2] Camden, quoted in Brand's *Antiquities*, vol. i. p. 227.
[3] Frazer, *op. cit.* vol. i. p. 78.
[4] *Ibid.* p. 77.

even with sausages, rolls of tobacco, rings, needles, etc.
Often bottles of wine or beer are also suspended to it.
It is known as the May, harvest-May, *bouquet de la
moisson*, and it is frequently set up in the field which
is in process of cutting. When the reaping is over it
is brought home on the last sheaf or on the last load,
or is borne by a harvestman seated on the waggon or
walking before it. On its arrival at the homestead it
is solemnly welcomed by the farmer, and attached to
some conspicuous spot on the barn or house. Here it
remains for a year until replaced by its successor.
Another feature of the ceremony, which is no doubt of
the nature of a rain charm, consists in the drenching of
the May and its bearers with water, or in the sprinkling
of them with wine. A variant of this observance is
met with in other parts of Europe, where at some date
after harvest the farmer causes a lofty pole, dressed
with ribbons and hung with handkerchiefs, articles of
clothing, cakes, fruit, etc., to be erected in his field.
The labourers then climb or race for the prizes.[1]

There can be no question as to the antiquity of
these customs. Mannhardt, who has carefully studied
the subject, finds a most remarkable similarity between
the harvest festivals of ancient Greece and those of
modern Europe. The *eiresione* or harvest-bush of the
Greeks, which is reproduced "with almost photographic
exactness" in the harvest-May above described,[2]
was a branch of olive or laurel, bound with red and
white wool, and hung with ribbons, the finest harvest-
fruits, cakes, and jars of honey, oil, and wine. It was
carried in solemn procession with choral songs, at the
Thargelia or feast of first-fruits in the late spring, and
at the Pyanepsia or true harvest-festival in the early

[1] Mannhardt II. p. 212.   [2] *Ibid.* p. 214.

autumn, its destination at the former festival being the temple of Athena Polias, at the latter that of Apollo. It was planted before the door of the temple, the contents of the jars attached to it were poured over it, and the following lines were sung: "*Eiresione* brings figs and plump loaves, and honey in jars, and oil wherewith to anoint yourself, and cups of wine unwatered, that you may drink yourself to sleep."[1] In addition to this official ceremony each landowner who grew corn and fruit held his own festival, the *eiresione* in that case being suspended or fastened before his house-door, or placed inside the house beside the ancestral images. There it remained for a twelvemonth, until on the bringing home of the next year's branch it was taken down and burnt. It was to this private *eiresione* that the familiar passages in Aristophanes allude. Demos hearing a noise at his front door, jumps to the conclusion that a street brawl is imminent: "Who's making that hullaballoo?" he cries; "away from my door. What, will ye tear down my *eiresione*?"[2] His dread is that his harvest-branch will be requisitioned as a weapon of offence, a possible application of it also alluded to by the poet in another passage.[3] Elsewhere it is jestingly said of a dried-up old woman, that if a spark fell on her, she would burn up like an old *eiresione*,[4] a comparison which throws light on the mode of disposing of the last year's branch.

The *Oschophoria*, or carrying in procession of the *oschos*, a vine-branch with the ripe grapes upon it, was another of the Athenian harvest festivals, and is interesting in the present connection from its being

---

[1] Bötticher, *op. cit.* p. 393.
[2] *Knights*, v. 729.
[3] *Wasps*, v. 398.
[4] *Plutus*, v. 1054.

associated, like some modern harvest observances, with a racing competition.

These festivals, which were probably of prehistoric origin, were in classical times sanctified for the popular mind by being linked with and accounted for by some legendary event which appealed to the patriotic sentiment. But in spite of this they would appear in course of time to have undergone something of the same debasement as our own May observances, and degenerated into a begging procession from door to door. At any rate the word *eiresione*, originally applied to the festival hymn as well as to the branch, became in later times the general name for all begging-songs. Initially, however, the *eiresione* was, no doubt, a symbolical representation of the genius of vegetation, and as such was addressed as a person.[1]

Traced to its remote origin, there can be little doubt that the ceremony of bringing in the May arose from a similar process of reasoning. The gods or spirits of those far-off times had their habitation, or at least manifested their activity, in the tree. The gifts of rain and sunshine were in their hands. They made the crops to grow, the herds to multiply, and women to give increase. According to Aeneas Sylvius, the Lithuanians believed that their sacred groves were the house of the god who gave them rain and sunshine.[2] In Circassia the pear-tree is still regarded as the protector of cattle, and in the autumn is cut down, carried home, and worshipped as a god.[3] In many countries trees are held to have the power of helping women in childbirth.[4] It was therefore no more unnatural for an ignorant peasantry to believe

[1] Mannhardt II. p. 257.
[2] Aeneas Sylvius, *Opera* (Bale, 1571), p. 418.
[3] Frazer, *op. cit.* vol. i. p. 73.
[4] *Ibid.* p. 74.

that the same power and influence existed in the cut branches of trees than it is for a modern uncultured Catholic to expect help from sacred relics. In each case the process of thought is the same. Eventually the ceremony of carrying the branch round the village, the primitive purpose of which was to make each house a sharer in the benevolent offices of the tree-spirit, degenerated into a meaningless observance, a pretext for indulging in festivities and levying contributions. But there can be no doubt that the securing of fertility and abundance, together with the supply of rain and sunshine necessary thereto, was originally the root-idea of the world-wide spring observances.

(2) The custom of setting up the May-pole on the village green had, no doubt, a similar genesis. It represented for the community what the May-day decoration of the house represented for the family. In parts of Europe the pole is sometimes planted in front of the Mayor's or Burgomaster's house.[1] The intention, evidently, was to bring to the village as a whole the newly-quickened generative spirit resident in the woods. The custom of cutting down a tree, decorating it with garlands and ribbons, re-erecting it, and fêting it with dance and song, has prevailed in almost every country in the world. In some instances it is further dressed as a mortal, or a human image is attached to it, as in the Attis rites, testifying to the anthropomorphic conception of the tree-spirit. The doll placed in the centre of the children's May garlands would seem to be a survival of this custom. The same feature of the celebration is illustrated most clearly in the Greek festival of the little Daedala, which may be

[1] Mannhardt I. p. 167.

regarded as "a classical equivalent of an English May-day in the olden time."[1] The festival was inaugurated in an ancient oak-forest. Cooked meat was placed upon the ground and the movements of the birds which came to feed upon it were carefully observed. The tree upon which a bird was first observed to alight with the meat in its bill was cut down, carved into the image of a woman, and dressed as a bride. It was then placed upon a cart and drawn in procession with singing and dancing. It must be added that Mr. Farnell regards this festival as a survival from prehistoric times of the processional ceremony of the "sacred marriage" between Zeus and Hera, which may possibly have been symbolical of the marriage of earth and heaven in spring.[2]

In the case of our own May-pole, it was originally, no doubt, the custom to erect a fresh tree every year, in order that the newly-awakened energy of the forest might be communicated to the village, and in many parts this feature of the custom appears to have survived, as we may gather from the Puritan accounts above quoted. Elsewhere, as the intention of the ceremony was lost sight of, a permanent May-pole was substituted for the annual tree, and was converted on May-day, by means of garlands and flowers, into the semblance of a living growth. The May-tree of the German village, for instance, is a permanent construction, made up of several tall trunks.[3] On May-day, cakes, sausages, eggs, and other desirable things are hung upon it, the villagers dance around it, and the young men climb it to secure its gifts. In some parts the May-pole is surmounted by a cross, and the

---

[1] Frazer, *op. cit.* vol. i. p. 100. [2] Farnell, *op. cit.* vol. i. pp. 185, 189.
[3] Mannhardt I. p. 169.

symbol of a dead faith is consecrated by that of a living one.

Yet the old faith long left its traces in several quaint observances. Amongst the Wends of the Elbe the cattle were driven every year round the village tree. The bride imported from another village must dance around it and pay it her footing. The wounded villager also gave it money and got himself healed by rubbing himself against it.[1] Such usages are only intelligible on the theory that the tree was once seriously believed to be the local habitation of a spirit, who concentrated in himself the marvellous fruitfulness and healing beneficence of nature.

The custom so often met with on the Continent[2] of attaching a young sapling or a branch to the roof of a house newly built, or in process of erection, is another survival, descended, no doubt, from the ancient belief in the benign influence of the tree-inhabiting spirit. In some places it is usual to decorate the bough with flowers, ribbons, and strings of eggs, which last are clearly intended to symbolise the life-giving power assumed to be the spirit's special attribute.

(3) But the conception which underlay and actuated the May celebrations is illustrated still more clearly by their third feature—the choice of a youth or maiden, or both, to personify the reawakened and rejoicing nature. A great deal of evidence on this subject has been collected by Mannhardt and Frazer, which can only be briefly summarised here. In the case of the begging processions with May-trees or May-boughs from door to door, it was once really believed that the good genius of growth was present unseen in

[1] Mannhardt I. p. 174. [2] *Ibid.* p. 218.

the bough. But often he was represented in addition by a man dressed in green leaves and flowers, or by a girl similarly adorned, who being looked upon as an actual representative of the spirit of vegetation, was supposed to produce the same beneficial effects on the fowls, the fruit-trees, and the crops as the presence of the deity himself. "The names May, Father May, May Lady, Queen of the May, by which the anthropomorphic spirit of vegetation is often denoted, show that the conception of the spirit of vegetation is blent with a personification of the season at which his powers are most strikingly manifested."[1]

In some cases the human representative of the tree-spirit goes hand in hand with his vegetable representative, the tree or branch. The former may be merely a doll or puppet, as in the Lady of the May of our own May garlands, or it may be a chosen youth or girl, who carries a miniature May-tree, or is throned beside the May-pole, or dances around it, clad in leafy garments. Sometimes the chief actor in the ceremony is ducked in a pond or drenched with water, or, as is still the case in some parts of Ireland, carries a pail of water and a mop to distribute its contents, with the idea of ensuring rain by a sort of sympathetic magic. In other cases the tree disappears from the celebration, and the whole burden of representing its indwelling spirit falls upon its human substitute, who in such event is almost always swathed in leaves or flowers. The Green George of Carinthia[2] and our own Jack-in-the-Green are instances of this custom. The pence collected no doubt represent what was once a willing contribution for services presumably useful and worthy of reward.

[1] Mannhardt I. p. 315. [2] *Ibid.* p. 313.

The custom of electing a King or Queen of the May is very general throughout Europe.¹ The original purpose was, no doubt, to personify the regal character of the spirit who ruled the woods, but in other cases the representative is termed a Bridegroom or Bride, emphasising another attribute of the deity. In England the crowning of the May-queen closed the long day's ceremonies, and the young people who had been up before sunrise to bring in the May, and had danced all day upon the village green, ended their pleasant labours at sundown with this graceful observance.

In some instances *two* representatives of the spirit of vegetation were chosen, under the names of King and Queen, or Prince and Princess, or Lord and Lady. The King and Queen are mentioned in an English document of the thirteenth century, and there is evidence to show that Robin Hood and Maid Marian were originally representatives of the vegetation spirit, for the former is spoken of in an old book of 1576 as King of the May, while Marian or May-Marian, as she was sometimes called, was certainly a Queen of May, and as such was represented wearing a golden crown and carrying in her hand a red pink, the emblem of summer.²

At the time when we first encounter them in history these celebrations had already lost their religious significance and passed into graceful observances, the excuse for innocent mirth. But if we trace them back into the gloom in which they arose we come upon evidence which seems to show that they were not always so innocent. It is quite probable that in very early times the human representative of

---

¹ Mannhardt I. pp. 341 *et seq.*
² Brand's *Antiquities*, vol. i. pp. 253-261.

the spirit of vegetation was actually sacrificed, in order that the divine spirit incarnate in him might be transferred in unabated vigour to his successor,[1] just as the old May-pole was destroyed and a new one set up in its place. Herein was typified the annual death and resurrection of the spirit of vegetation, a conception which has given rise to many celebrations, not always free from bloodshed, in different parts of the world. The rites by which in Egypt and Western Asia the death and resurrection of Osiris, Adonis, Tammuz, Attis, and Dionysus were solemnised find their parallels not only in the barbarous usages once current in Mexico, but also in certain spring and summer celebrations of the peasants of Europe.

The Mexican god of the plant-world was Huitzilopochtli, and at the feast of Teteionan, mother of the gods, a woman clothed as the goddess was sacrificed, her head cut off, and her skin used to dress a youth, who was then taken to the god's temple, accompanied by a large crowd of worshippers.[2] That is to say, the old embodiment of plant life was killed, and its personality, typified by the skin, was given to a youthful successor, who, doubtless, was sacrificed in his turn when it was considered necessary for the health of the plant-world.

In some modern European spring observances the actual putting to death of the spirit of vegetation survives in symbol. "In Lower Bavaria, the Whitsuntide representative of the tree-spirit — the Pfingstl, as he is called — was clad from top to toe in leaves and flowers. On his head he wore a high pointed cap, the ends of which rested on his shoulders, only two holes being left for his eyes. The

---

[1] Frazer, *op. cit.* vol. i. p. 240.   [2] Mannhardt I. p. 360.

cap was covered with water-flowers and surmounted with a nosegay of peonies. The sleeves of his coat were also made of water-plants, and the rest of his body was enveloped in alder and hazel leaves. On each side of him marched a boy, holding up one of the Pfingstl's arms. These two boys carried drawn swords, and so did most of the others who formed the procession. They stopped at every house where they hoped to receive a present, and the people in hiding soused the leaf-clad boy with water. All rejoiced when he was well drenched. Finally he waded into the brook up to his middle, whereupon one of the boys, standing on the bridge, pretended to cut off his head."[1]

"At Wurmlingen in Swabia a score of young fellows dress themselves on Whit-Monday in white shirts and white trousers with red scarves round their waists, and swords hanging from the scarves. They ride on horseback into the wood, led by two trumpeters blowing their trumpets. In the wood they cut down leafy oak branches, in which they envelope from head to foot him who was the last of their number to ride out of the village. His legs, however, are encased separately, so that he may be able to mount his horse again. Further, they give him a long artificial neck, with an artificial head and a false face on the top of it. Then a May-tree is cut, generally an aspen or beech about ten feet high; and being decked with coloured handkerchiefs and ribbons, it is entrusted to a special 'May-bearer.' The cavalcade then returns, with music and song, to the village. Amongst the personages who figure in the procession are a Moorish king with a sooty face and crown on his head, a Dr.

[1] Frazer, *op. cit.* vol. i. p. 241.

Iron-Beard, a corporal, and an executioner. They halt on the village green, and each of the characters makes a speech in rhyme. The executioner announces that the leaf-clad man has been condemned to death, and cuts off his false head. Then the riders race to the May-tree, which has been set up a little way off. The first man who succeeds in wrenching it from the ground as he gallops past keeps it with all its decorations. The ceremony is observed every second or third year."[1]

In Saxony and Thuringia, at Whitsuntide, the Wild Man, a person disguised in branches and moss, was chased through the woods. On being overtaken he was shot at with blank cartridge and pretended to fall down dead. A mock doctor then bled him and he soon came to life again. The rejoicing people placed him in a waggon, and led him about in procession, to receive gifts at the houses of the village.[2]

The common feature in all these apparently senseless observances is the symbolical sacrifice of the human representative of the spirit of vegetation, and they drive us to the conclusion that there was a time when the victim was sacrificed in reality. In the same way the custom still current in Belgium and French Flanders at the summer festival of drawing in procession large wicker figures enclosing living men, recalls the gigantic images of ozier-work, covered with leaves, in which the Druids confined the victims destined for their fiery sacrifices.[3]

---

[1] Frazer, *op. cit.* vol. i. p. 242. [2] *Ibid.* vol. i. p. 243.
[3] Mannhardt I. p. 523.

CHAPTER IX

CHRISTMAS OBSERVANCES

In modern times, as the once joyful celebrations of May-day have waned the festivities of Christmas-tide have undergone increase and development. The grosser features of the festival have, no doubt, been eliminated; the mummers and the lord of misrule have for the most part gone the way of the May-king, but all the more graceful and orderly observances of the time have strengthened their hold on the popular favour. The decoration of the house is as usual to-day at Christmas as it once was at May-day, and the Christmas-tree has stepped into the place which the May-tree once held in the affections of the young. Yet if we trace these Christmas observances back to their origin, we find them as distinctively pagan in their ancestry as the festivities of May-day.

We owe the survival of many pagan customs largely to the Roman Church, whose settled policy it was to adapt the old festal rites to the purposes of the new faith, and to divert its rude converts from the riotous festivities of their unconverted friends by offering them the more orderly rejoicings of a Christian holy day. Gregory the Great, when he sent his missionaries to Britain, instructed them to Christianise the festivals and temples of the heathen, "raising their stubborn minds upwards not by leaps, but step by step." And Dr. Tille, in his learned work on the German Christmas,[1] has shown what pains were taken by the priesthood to transfer to their own feast the rude rejoicings with which the unconverted Germans celebrated their great festival at the beginning of winter. The same transference of pre-Christian usages occurred in Italy, where the Christmas festival, first definitely fixed at the time of the winter solstice by Bishop Liberius, A.D. 354,[2] inherited, as expressly stated by Polydore Virgil, several of the features of the great Roman festival of the Saturnalia, held about the same time. This festival was an occasion for universal mirth and festivity. Friends visited and feasted each other, and there was a general interchange of presents, the objects presented consisting usually of branches, wax tapers, and clay dolls. The stalls were laden with gifts, like the Christmas shops of to-day. One of the days of the festival, the *dies juvenalis*, was devoted to children. The solstitial character of the festival is shown by the fact that another of its days was dedicated by the Emperor Aurelian to the Persian sun-god, Mithra; and Varro states that the clay dolls, which were an important feature of the celebration, represented the infant sacrifices once made to a Phoenician Baal who had been introduced to Rome under the name of Saturn or Cronos.[3]

However this may be, it is clear that some observances familiar to us at Christmas—the feasting, the present giving, and the now obsolete mumming—have an origin which is lost in antiquity. Other customs,

[1] Alexander Tille, *Die Geschichte der Deutschen Weihnacht* (Leipzig, 1893).
[2] *Ibid.* p. 2.
[3] J. G. Frazer in *Encyclop. Brit.*, 9th edition, vol. xxi. p. 321.

too, though with a different *provenance*, have an equally venerable ancestry. The use of mistletoe, for instance, is without doubt a direct legacy from the Druids, who were wont at the time of the solstices solemnly to place upon their altars the mysterious branch, into which it was thought that the spirit of the tree retreated when the rest of the leaves had fallen. This practice, strangely enough, survived until within comparatively recent years in a ceremonial practised at York Minster and some other northern churches,[1] though as a rule the introduction of the mistletoe into Christian edifices was strongly reprobated, on the score that it was a heathen emblem.

The practice of decorating the house at the New Year with holly and other evergreens was also a pagan observance. Dr. Chandler refers to it as a Druidic custom, the intention being to provide the sylvan spirits with a shelter to which they might repair, "and remain unnipped with frost and cold winds, until a milder season had renewed the foliage of their darling abodes."[2] In early times the Church made a stand against this use of evergreens as being a pagan custom, but the interdict was not persevered in, and later on we find the decoration of the churches a recognised practice, the note for Christmas eve in the old Calendar being, *Templa exornantur.*[3]

The observance, however, which most concerns us here is that of the Christmas-tree, the evolution of which furnishes us with one of the most interesting chapters in the history of religious development. To the present generation the Christmas-tree appears such an essential feature of the festival, as celebrated in this

[1] W. Stukeley, *Medallic History of Carausius* (1757-59), vol. ii. pp. 163, 164.
[2] Brand's *Antiquities*, vol. i. p. 520.
[3] *Ibid.* pp. 519, 521.

country, that many will be surprised to hear how recent an importation it is. But as a matter of fact, the Christmas-tree was practically unknown in England until it was introduced by the late Prince Consort.[1] Even in Germany, the land of its origin, it was not universally established as an integral part of the festival until the beginning of the present century,[2] and it was only at that date that it came to be known as the "Weihnachtsbaum" and "Christbaum."[3] Goethe in 1774 describes it as adorned with wax tapers, sweetmeats, and apples, but calls it simply the "decorated tree."[4] Schiller in 1789 finds no more distinctive name for it than the "green tree."[5] Since that time, or rather since 1830, its diffusion throughout the world has been so marvellously rapid that there is nothing to compare with it in the whole history of popular customs.

In Germany the Christmas-tree can be traced back more or less in its present form to the beginning of the seventeenth century, when an unnamed writer, in some extremely fragmentary notes, tells us that it was the custom at Strasburg to set up fir-trees in the houses at Christmas, and to deck them with roses of coloured paper, apples, etc.[6] The next mention of it occurs half a century later in the writings of Professor Dannhauer, a celebrated theologian, also living in Strasburg.[7] "Amongst the other absurdities," he writes, "with which men are often more busied at Christmas than with the Word of God, there is also the Christmas or fir-tree, which they erect in their houses,

---

[1] Mannhardt I. p. 240.
[2] *Ibid.* p. 238.
[3] Tille, *op. cit.* p. 264.
[4] Goethe, *Die Leiden des jungen Werthers* (Am 20 December).
[5] Schiller und Lotte (Stuttgart, 1856), p. 574.
[6] Tille, *op. cit.* p. 258.
[7] *Ibid.* p. 259.

hang it with dolls and sweetmeats, and then shake it and cause it to shed its flowers. I know not the origin of the custom, it is a child's game. . . . Far better were it to lead the children to the spiritual cedar, Christ Jesus." The reprobation of the Strasburg preacher was echoed by other divines, and to this cause probably the Christmas-tree owed its slow diffusion throughout Germany. The theological dislike of it, however, as it turned out, was ill-advised, for eventually the Christmas-tree displaced other popular observances of a far less innocent nature.

So far we have been treading historical ground, but in tracing the Christmas-tree still farther back we have only inference to go upon. The subject, however, has been carefully worked out by Dr. Tille,[1] and the pedigree which he traces for the tree is a most interesting one. His argument must here be condensed as closely as possible. The Christmas-tree, with its lights, its artificial flowers, and its apples and other fruit, is presumably connected with the legend of Christmas flowering trees, which was very familiar to the Middle Ages, and of which the English myth of the Glastonbury thorn is an example. The origin of the legend in Germany is thus explained by Dr. Tille: —It is not unusual when the season is mild to find trees blossoming in November, especially the cherry and the crab-tree. For the old German peasant the New Year began with the great slaughtering feast early in November, when the cattle were brought in from the pastures, and all the superfluous ones were butchered and feasted on; the winter was thus counted to the New Year, like the eve to a holy day. Hence when trees blossomed late, a casual connection was inevitably

[1] Tille, *op. cit.* chap. viii.

traced between the strange phenomenon and the New Year feast at which it took place. On the introduction of Christianity the feasts of St. Martin, St. Andrew, and St. Nicholas were substituted for the ancient festivals. The strange blossoming power of nature was connected with St. Andrew's Day, and fruit-boughs severed on that day were believed by the people to possess particular virtue.[1] The Mediaeval Church, always eager to enlist popular superstitions in its own support, set itself to transfer to Christmas the blossoming tree of the November festival, and the legends which related how celebrated magicians like Albertus Magnus, Paracelsus, and Faustus had made for themselves a summer in the heart of winter were incorporated by the monks into the lives of certain saints.[2] The belief in trees that blossomed and bore fruit at Christmas was widely distributed and firmly held amongst the people in the later Middle Ages. In the German literature of the fifteenth and sixteenth centuries many instances of the miraculous fact are circumstantially recorded.[3] A writer in 1430 relates that "not far from Nuremburg there stood a wonderful tree. Every year, in the coldest season, on the night of Christ's birth this tree put forth blossoms and apples as thick as a man's thumb. This in the midst of deep snow and in the teeth of cold winds." In a MS. letter of the Bishop of Bamberg, dated 1426, and preserved in the Hofbibliothek at Vienna, the actual blossoming of two apple-trees at Christmas is mentioned as an acknowledged fact, and we find a Protestant preacher giving full credence to the belief nearly a couple of centuries later.

But the most striking instance of the hold which

[1] Tille, *op. cit.* p. 220.   [2] *Ibid.* p. 221.   [3] *Ibid.* p. 226.

such legends had taken on the popular mind is to be found in connection with our own miraculous tree, the Glastonbury Thorn—

> The winter thorn
> Which blossoms at Christmas, mindful of our Lord.

This tree, which was the object of such veneration in the later Middle Ages that the merchants of Bristol are said to have found the export of its blossoms extremely remunerative, stood upon an eminence near the town of Glastonbury. The legend ran that Joseph of Arimathea, who, according to monkish teaching, was the first Christian missionary to this country, one Christmas eve planted his staff in the ground. The staff, which years previously had been cut from a hawthorn-tree, at once took root and put forth leaves, and by the next day was in full blossom. The miracle was repeated on every subsequent Christmas-day. Even after the Reformation we find King James I. and his queen and other persons of quality giving large sums for cuttings from the tree, which were believed to have the same miraculous virtue as the parent thorn, and even in the following reign it was customary to carry a branch of the tree in procession and present it to the king. In the Civil War the original tree was destroyed, but some of its off-shoots survived, one especially at Quainton in Buckinghamshire, which suddenly sprang into fame again when the new style was introduced into the Calendar in 1752, and the people, resenting the loss of their eleven days, appealed from the decision of their rulers to the higher wisdom of the miraculous tree. According to the *Gentleman's Magazine* for 1753, about two thousand people on the night of 24th December 1752 came with lanthorns and candles to view the thorn-tree, "which was remembered (this year only) to be a slip from the Glastonbury thorn." As the tree remained bare the people agreed that 25th December, N.S., could not be the true Christmas-day, and refused to celebrate it as such. Their excitement was intensified when on 5th January the tree was found to be in full bloom, and to pacify them the authorities were driven to decree that the old Christmas-day should be celebrated as well as the new. It may be added that two thorn-trees still exist near the ruins of Glastonbury Abbey, which blossom during the winter, and are identified by Loudoun with a variety of hawthorn, the *Crataegus oxyacantha praecox*, which is admittedly a winter flowerer.[1]

There is, however, as Mannhardt points out,[2] another way in which a fruit-bearing tree became popularly associated with Christmas. The ancient Church had devoted the day before Christmas-day to the memory of Adam and Eve, and it was customary at Christmas in many parts of the Continent to give a dramatic representation of the story of the Creation and Fall in connection with the drama of the Nativity. Hence arose the Paradise-plays which were familiar to the Middle Ages from the thirteenth century onward. The well-known legend that the cross of Christ was fashioned from a tree which had sprung from a slip of the Tree of Knowledge served as a link between the events celebrated so closely together, the Fall and the Birth of the Redeemer, and gave additional significance to the scenery of the Paradise-play, consisting, as it usually did, of trees, or sometimes of a single tree, laden with apples and decked with ribbons. In

---

[1] Folkard, *op. cit.* pp. 352, 353.   [2] Mannhardt I. p. 242.

some cases the tree was carried on to the stage by one of the actors. In this way the apple-bearing tree became the recognised scenic symbol of Christmas, and naturally connected itself with, if it did not spring out of, the very early legend of the Church that all nature blossomed at the birth of Christ, who Himself, according to the fanciful symbolism of the time, was the very Tree of Life which had once stood in paradise.

Another popular custom, which dates back to the time when the belief in the beneficent power of sylvan deities was general, is also probably entitled to a place in the pedigree of the Christmas-tree. It was customary amongst the ancient Germans on one of the sacred nights of the winter festival, when, according to the popular belief, nature was permeated with new life, to cut wands from the hedges.[1] These were brought home, put in water or planted in a pot of moist earth, and solemnly placed, some in the open air, some in the stable, and some in the house. A month later each wand would be in full bloom, and it was then the custom to carry it round and lightly strike with it those to whom one wished to impart health, strength, and fruitfulness. Those struck with it rewarded the striker with presents, in recompense for the benefit he was assumed to convey. This custom, which is probably of Indian origin, survived in some parts of the Continent as a child's game even in the present century. Under the influence of Christianity the day for cutting the wands was delayed, so that they might bloom at Christmas, and in some parts it is still usual to arrange that there shall be a flowering branch in the house at that time. In Nordlingen, a century ago, families used to compete with each other as to which

[1] Tille, *op. cit.* p. 244.

should be able to show the most flourishing branch at Christmas-tide.[1] To this day in Austrian Silesia the peasant women sally forth at midnight on St. Andrew's eve to pluck a branch from an apricot-tree. It is put in water and flowers about Christmas time, and is taken by them to Mass on Christmas-day.[2]

Amongst people to whom the apple-bearing tree of the Paradise-play was familiar the substitution for the blooming branch of an evergreen decked with fruits and ribbons and artificial flowers was quite natural. It became, as it were, a proxy for the deciduous branch, still remaining the occasion for present-giving, though now the tree became the giver instead of the receiver of gifts.

The custom of hanging lights upon the Christmas-tree is a comparatively late innovation, the well-known print of "Christmas in Luther's Home," where an illuminated fir-tree is represented as the centre of the festivity, being demonstrably an anachronism. The Christmas-tree, when we first definitely meet with it at the beginning of the seventeenth century, was certainly not illuminated. But the idea of a light-bearing tree was familiar to the Middle Ages. An old Icelandic legend relates that once upon a time, at Mödhrufell, there stood a mountain-ash which had sprung from the blood of two innocent persons who had been executed there.[3] Every Christmas-eve the tree was seen to be covered with lights, which the strongest gale could not extinguish. These lights were its wonderful blossoms, for in folk-lore lights are often made to represent flowers and *vice-versâ*.[4] In the old French legend of Perceval, the hero is represented as coming upon a

[1] Tille, *op. cit.* p. 249.
[2] *Ibid.* p. 250.
[3] Mannhardt I. p. 241.
[4] Mannhardt *Germanische Mythen* (Berlin, 1858), p. 470, note.

tree illuminated with a thousand candles, and Durmals le Galois, another hero of mediaeval legend, twice saw a magnificent tree covered with lights from top to bottom.¹

It has already been mentioned that wax-tapers were given as presents at the Roman Saturnalia, and it may well be that the connection of lighted candles with Christmas time may date back to the ancient solstitial celebrations, in which they were regarded as symbolical of the new birth of the sun. The same idea—that of typifying the renewal of life by means of lighted tapers—is found in the Netherlands in connection with the May-tree, which there bears lights amongst its other decorations. At Venlo on the Maas the maidens light the tapers as the evening comes on and then dance around the lighted tree.² At Lüneberg, at wedding festivities, it is usual to carry a "May" adorned with lights before the bridal pair, and in the Hartz Mountains the so-called "St. John's tree," round which the peasants dance, is a pyramid adorned with wreaths, flowers, and lights.

In all these customs, which are no doubt survivals of the belief in a tree-inhabiting deity, we see the collateral relations, if not the direct progenitors of our Christmas-tree. In short, modern as it is in its present form, the Christmas-tree epitomises many most ancient ideas; is the point to which many streams converge whose source is hidden in a far distant antiquity. It is the meeting-point of the old pagan belief in the virtues vested in the tree and of the quaint fancies of the Middle Ages, which loved to see spiritual truths embodied in material forms. Christ, the Tree of Life, blossoming on Christmas-eve

Tille, *op. cit.* p. 220.   ² Mannhardt I. p. 244.

in Mary's bosom; the fatal tree of paradise whence sprang the cross, the instrument of man's salvation,—that " fruit-bearing heavenly-nourished tree planted in the midst of redeemed man," so often represented in mediaeval art; the miracle of nature, so stirred by the wonder of the event as to break forth into blossom in the midst of winter—all these ideas, so characteristic of mediaeval thought, became grafted together with observances derived from solstitial worship, upon the stock of the sacred tree, laden with offerings and decked with fillets. Indeed the Christmas-tree may be said to recapitulate the whole story of tree-worship,—the May-tree, the harvest-tree, the Greek *eiresione*, the tree as the symbol and embodiment of deity, and last but not least, the universe-tree, bearing the lights of heaven for its fruit and covering the world with its branches.

INDEX

ACACIA, the, 11, 39, 40, 45
Accadians, the, 2, 4, 6, 111, 133
Acis, metamorphosis of, 81
Adonis, 11, 75, 81, 159
Aesculapius, laurel sacred to, 37
Alexander the Great, and the flower-maidens, 60; and the Persian tree-oracles, 99
Ama-ravati, Buddhist sculptures at, 14
Ambrosia, 126
America, tree-worship in, 16, 17
Amrita, 125
Aphrodite, 30, 32, 46, 81, 88; apples sacred to, 37; myrtle sacred to, 37
Apollo, 47, 76, 98, 99; and Daphne, 77; laurel sacred to, 36, 47, 50, 77
Apples, sacred to Aphrodite, 37; of Hesperides, 119
Arabia, the *jinni* of, 24, 52, 54, 94; tree-oracles in, 99, 102; tree-worship in, 45
Argo, oracular beam of the, 98
Armenia, tree-oracles in, 99; use of branches in, 49
Artemis, 49, 76; a vegetation deity, 29, 88; sacred tree of, 45, 49
Ashêra, the, 8, 88, 96
Assyria, tree-worship in, 5, 6, 88
Astarte, 8, 30, 87; the cypress sacred to, 40
Athena, 152; the olive sacred to, 38
Athens, festivals at, 48, 151
Atlantis, the lost, 139
Atlas, Mount, 110, 119, 135, 136
Attis, a tree-god, 11, 75, 80, 81, 154, 159
Auxerre, sacred tree of, 20
Avalon, the isle of, 140

BABYLONIA, tree-worship in, 6; mountain worship in, 112; world-tree of, 111
Banian, the, 42, 64, 76
Basil, Holy, of India, 43
Baucis and Philemon, metamorphosis of, 79
Bavaria, Whitsuntide custom in, 159
Beech, the sacred, 46
Bharhut, Buddhist sculptures at, 15, 40, 42
Bo-tree, the, 40, 116
Bodhi-trees of the Buddhas, 40
Borneo, tree-worship in, 16
Bötticher, general conclusion of, regarding tree-worship, 21
Brahma, 14, 43, 115
Branches forced into flower at Christmas, 170; religious use of, 13, 36, 37, 38, 47, 48, 91
Brittany, use of laurel branch in, 91
Buddhas, the Bodhi-trees of the, 40
Buddhism, tree-worship and, 14, 40, 110, 116, 142
Burma, tree worship in, 16; tree-spirits of, 65

CANAAN, tree-worship in, 3, 8, 88; tree-oracles in, 95
Canute forbids tree-worship, 20
Carinthia, Green George of, 157
Cedar, the sacred, 7, 39, 40, 90, 95
Centaurs, the, 55, 56
Ceres, sacred grove of, 63
Chaldaea, cosmogony of, 113; demons of, 53; divination in, 105; illustrious mounds of, 112; oracles of, 95, 99; tree-worship in, 4, 6; world-tree of, 111

Charlemagne destroys the Irmensûl, 120
China, divination in, 105; legends of, 83; paradise legends of, 133; tree-worship in, 15; world-tree of, 118
Christmas observances, 162 *et seq.*
Christmas-tree, introduction into England, of, 165; origin in Germany of, 165
Churches, decoration of, at Christmas, 164
Circassia, pear-tree worshipped in, 153
Clymene, the daughters of, 78
Clytia, metamorphosis of, 80
Columbus and the earthly paradise, 141
Cronos, 163; a vegetation deity, 29
Cybele, 12, 30, 75, 81
Cyclops, the, 55, 56
Cypress, the sacred, 5, 13, 17, 39, 40, 51, 89, 131

Damaras, creation legend of the, 74
Daphne, 94; metamorphosis of, 77
Daphnephoria, the, 47
Delphi, sacred laurel of, 36, 47, 50, 77, 98; oracle of, 36, 50, 77, 94, 98, 102
Didû, the, emblem of Osiris, 34, 117
Dionysus, fruit-tree dressed as, 31, 33; sacred tree of, 27; a tree deity, 11, 12, 31, 32, 39, 48, 49, 57, 126, 159
Divination in Germany, 102; by leaves, 107; by roots, 106; in Sarmatia, 102; in Scythia, 102; in Sweden, 105
Divining rod, the, 103 *et seq.*
Dodona, oracular oak of, 28, 36, 93, 96, 98, 102
Druids, the, 20, 35, 103, 105, 161, 164
Dryads, the, 55, 58, 63
Dusares and the vine, 40

Ea, 7, 95, 111; sacred cedar of, 40, 131
Eddas, the, account of man's origin in, 73; description of Yggdrasil in, 112
Egypt, sacred sycamores of, 9, 25, 27, 44, 45; tree-demons of, 55; tree-worship in, 9, 10, 25, 45; world-tree of, 110, 117
Eiresione, the, 48, 151, 173; addressed as a person, 153

Elves, 24, 52, 63, 65
England, Christmas-tree in, 165; May celebrations in, 144 *et seq.*; tree-worship in, 20
Esdras, paradise of, 131
Esthonia, tree-worship in, 19, 44; world-tree of, 122

Fairies, the, 65
Fauns, the, 55, 58
Faunus, grove oracles of, 100
Fertility, the tree as genius of, 87, 153
Ficus ruminalis, the, 76, 86
Fig-tree, the, associated with the silvani, 58; carved as Pan, 33; spirit of, 58
Finland, tree-spirits of, 70; tree-worship in, 19; world-tree of, 120
Flower-maidens, the, 60
France, divination in, 105; harvest custom in, 150; tree-worship in, 19

Gautama, 14, 41, 43, 76, 116; and the Indian shot, 82
Germany, autumn festival in, 163, 166, 170; Christmas-tree in, 165; divination in, 102, 105; May customs in, 150, 155; tree-demons of, 19, 66; tree-worship in, 18
Gilgames, 119, 137
Gilgit, sacred cedar of, 90
Glastonbury thorn, the, 166, 168
God, the, and the tree, 24 *et seq.*
Gods, food of the, 113, 114, 122
Greece, creation legends of, 74; harvest customs of, 151; paradise legends of, 131; tree-worship in, 12, 17, 28, 46
Green ladies, the, 68

Hamadryads, the, 57, 58
Haoma, 13, 123, 130
Harvest May, the, 151, 173
Hâthor, a tree-goddess, 9, 10, 25
Helen, sacred tree of, 18, 31
Hera, 29, 32, 76, 155
Hermes, 79; birth of, 76
Hesperides, trees of the, 101, 119, 136

Iceland, paradise legend of, 138
India, paradise legend of, 129; soma ritual of, 124; tree-worship in, 13,

14, 35, 40, 43, 64; world-tree of, 115
Indra, the paradise of, **129**; and the soma, 125
Irmensûl, the, **120**
Israelites, tree-worship amongst, 3, 8; use of branches by, 48
Istar, 6, 8, 30, 88
Italy, modern belief in wood-spirits in, 58; tree-oracles in, 100; tree-worship in, **12**, 17, 28, 37, 47

JACK-IN-THE-GREEN, 148, 157
Japan, legends of, 83, 84; paradise legend of, 141; tree-demons of, 70; tree-worship in, **15**; world-tree of, 118
Jinni of Arabia, the, 24, 52, 54, 94

LAUREL, the sacred, 36, 47, 50, 59, 77, 91, 98
Life-rood, the (Lebensrute), 103, 127, 170
Life, the tree of, **15**, 130, 131, 142, 170
Life-tree, the, 84, 101
Little Daedala, festival of the, 155
Ljeschi, 69

MAHOMETAN paradise, the, 132, 134
Maid Marian, **158**
Maundeville, Sir J., his account of paradise, 137; his description of a tree of paradise, 143
May-bride, the, 158
May celebrations, 21, 145 *et seq.*
"May," the, 149, 151, 153
May-pole, the, 146, 154, 155
May queen, the, 146, 156
Melcarth, the cypress sacred to, 40
Melus, metamorphosis of, 80
Metamorphosis into trees, 77 *et seq.*
Metempsychosis into trees, 82 *et seq.*
Mexico, human sacrifices in, **159**; tree-symbol found in, 16; tree-worship in, 17
Milton, his description of paradise, 135
Mistletoe, 20, 164
Mithra, 13, 40, 163
Moss-women, the, 67
Myrtle, the sacred, **13**, 29, 37, 39, 86
Mulberry-tree, the, 96

NAKHLA, sacred acacia of, 45
Nantes, tree-worship condemned by Council of, 20
Narcissus, metamorphosis of, 81
Nejrân, sacred palm of, 45, 99
New Zealand, cosmogonic legend of, 110
Nicaragua, tree-worship in, 17
Nûît, a tree-goddess, 10, 25, 27, **117**; goddess of the sky, 110, 117

OAK, the sacred, of Ceres, 63; of the Druids, 20; of Esthonia, **122**; of Finland, 19, 44, **121**; of Pan, 56; of the Roman Capitol, **25**; at Romove, 44; of Zeus, 28, 35, 37, 93, 96, **101**, 155
Olive, the, sacred to Athena, 38; venerated by the Semites, 39, 49
Olympus, 134
Omens, tree, 101
Oracle-lots, 102
Oracles, tree, 93 *et seq.*
Origin-myths, 73
Oschophoria, the, 48, 152
Osiris, his emblem, the Didû or Tât, 34, 117; a tree-god, 11, 40, 159

PALESTINE, tree-demons of, 54; tree-worship in, 7, 8
Palm-tree, the, 5, 45, 49, 88, 99
Pan, a tree-god, 31, 33, 46, 56; the pipe of, 81
Paradise, 128 *et seq.*; an artificial, 143; the earthly, 136; trees of, 131, 142, 170
Paradise-plays, mediaeval, 169, 171
Patagonia, tree-worship in, 17
Pear-tree, the, worshipped in Circassia, 153
Permians, trees worshipped by the, 19
Persia, creation legends of, 23, 130; haoma ritual of, 123; tree-oracle in, 99; tree-worship in, 13, 123; use of branches in, 49; world-tree of, 115, 142
Peru, wood-ghost of, 71
Pfingstl, the, 159
Phyllis, metamorphosis of, 79
Pine, the sacred, 28, 31, 56, 58, 59, 80; venerated by the Semites, 39
Pippala, the, associated with Brahma, 14; with Gautama, 41
Plane-tree, the, of Armavira, 99; its connection with Pelops, 86; with Persian kings, 13

Poland, tree-worship in, 19
Pomegranate, the, 5, 30, 80
Poplar, the, sacred to Dis, 39; Zeus born beneath, 76
Puritans, denunciation of May-poles by, 21, 146

ROBIN HOOD, king of the May, 158
Rome, grove oracle in, 100; tree-worship in, 17, 28, 47
Romove, sacred oak of, 44
Russia, tree-demons of, 19, 66, 69; tree-worship in, 19; Whitsuntide custom in, 150

ST. MARK'S, Venice, symbol of sacred tree in, 2, 5, 7
Sânchi, Buddhist sculptures at, 14, 42
Sanctuary, the tree as, 49
Sarmatia, divination in, 102
Saturnalia, the, 163, 172
Satyrs, the, 55, 56, 57
Scandinavia, world-tree of, 112
Scythia, divination in, 102
Seïrīm, "Satyrs" of the Bible, 54
Semites, tree-oracles of the, 95; tree-worship amongst the, 7, 39-87
Sia Indians, cosmogony of, 118
Siam, tree-worship in, 16
Sileni, the, 55, 56
Silvanus, 28, 57
Sioux, creation legend of, 74
Soma, 124, 126
Sudan, tree-worship in the, 10
Sumatra, tree-worship in, 16
Swabia, spring observances in, 160
Sweden, divination in, 105; May observances in, 150; tree-spirits of, 68
Switzerland, tree-demons of, 68
Sycamores, the sacred, of Egypt, 9, 25, 27, 44, 45, 118

TAARA, a tree-god, 44
Talmud, the, paradise of, 132; life-tree mentioned in, 85
Tammuz, 6, 11, 12, 111, 159
Tapio, 70
Tât-pillar, the, 34, 117
Tengus of Japan, the, 70
Travancore, sacred tree in, 14
Tree, the, births beneath, 76; Chaldaean symbol of the sacred, 2, 5, 30, 88; dressed or carved as anthropo-morphic god, 27, 31, 32, 35, 103; of the community, 86, 154; of the family, 86, 101; of life, 15, 130, 131, 142, 170; lights on, 91, 171; offerings to, 30, 45, 46; of paradise, 131, 169; in relation to human life, 72; as symbol of fertility, 88; of universe, 109 *et seq.*, 173
Tree-deities, 9, 16, 24 *et seq.*
Tree-demons, 16, 24, 52, 55 *et seq.*
Tree-nymphs, 55, 56, 58, 59, 61, 62
Tree-oracles, 93 *et seq.*
Tree-origins, 73 *et seq.*
Tree-omens, 101
Tree-sanctuaries, 49
Tree-soul, the generalised, 90; primitive conception of, 1
Tree-worship, in Africa, 11; in America, 16, 17; in Arabia, 45; in Assyria, 6; in Borneo, 16; in Burma, 16; in Canaan, 3, 8; in Chaldaea, 4, 6, 111; in China, 15; in Egypt, 9, 10, 25, 45; in England, 20; in Esthonia, 19; in France, 19; in Finland, 19; in Germany, 18; in Greece, 17, 28, 46; in India, 13, 14, 35, 40, 43, 64, 124; in Japan, 15; in Mexico, 17; in Nicaragua, 17; in Palestine, 3, 7, 8; in Patagonia, 17; in Persia, 13, 123; in Phoenicia, 8, 12; in Phrygia, 12; in Poland, 19; in Rome, 17, 46; in Russia, 19; in the Semitic area, 7, 39, 87; in Siam, 16; in the Sudan, 11; in Sumatra, 16; origin of, 22
Trees, Christmas flowering, 116; legends of bleeding, 62, 63; legends of speaking, 101
Tristram and Iseult, legend of, 82
Trophonius, oracle of, 94
Tylor, Mr. E. B., on tree-worship, 21
Tyrol, wild women of, 67

UPSALA, sacred grove of, 43

VINE-WOMEN of Lucian, the, 60
Vine, the, sacred to Dionysus, 39; to Dusares, 40; venerated by the Semites, 39
Vishnu, 43, 76

"WEGE-WARTE," legend of the, 83
Wends, the, and the May-pole, 156
Wild-fanggen, the, 67

INDEX

Wild men of the woods, 21, 52, 56, 66, 68, 71, 161

Willow, the, connected with Artemis, 29; with Hera, 29, 76; inhabited by tree-spirit, 62

Woden, 43

Wood-maidens, 67

World-mountain, the, 110, 112, 118, 134

World-tree, the, 109 *et seq.*; of Buddhists, 116; of Chaldaea, 111; of Egypt, 110, 117; of Esthonia, 122; of Finland, 120; of India, 115; of Persia, 115; of Scandinavia, 112

YGGDRASIL, 112 *et seq.*

ZEUS, a tree-god, 18, 28, **29**, **35**, **46**, 155; oracle of, at Dodona, **93**, **96**

Zeus-Ammon, oracle **of, 96**

THE END

Printed by R. & R. CLARK, LIMITED, *Edinburgh.*

www.ingramcontent.com/pod-product-compliance
Lightning Source LLC
Chambersburg PA
CBHW032135160426
43197CB00008B/647